IT COULD
HAPPEN
HERE

IT COULD HAPPEN HERE

AMERICA ON THE BRINK

BRUCE JUDSON

HARPER

An Imprint of HarperCollinsPublishers
www.harpercollins.com

HarperCollins books may be purchased for educational, business, or sales promotional use. For information, please write: Special Markets Department, HarperCollins Publishers, 10 East 53rd Street, New York, NY 10022.

FIRST EDITION

Designed by William Ruoto

Library of Congress Cataloging-in-Publication Data

Judson, Bruce.
    It could happen here : America on the brink / Bruce Judson.
1st ed.
        p.   cm.
    ISBN 978-0-06-168910-9
    1. Distributive justice—United States. 2. Income distribution—United States. 3. Wealth—United States. 4. Revolutions—Economic aspects—United States. I. Title.
HB523.J83   2009
339.20973—dc22   2009018296

---

09 10 11 12 13   OV/RRD   10 9 8 7 6 5 4 3 2 1

This book is dedicated to my wife, Nancy Gayle Judson, who makes all things possible.

ACKNOWLEDGMENTS

To attempt to write about the meaning of the large trends in our society, and their potential impact on our future, is a forbidding task. As a consequence, this book, more than most, owes its existence to the support, insights, and assistance of many people.

First and foremost, I would like to thank my editor, Bruce Nichols, who, from the outset of the project, was enthusiastic about bringing my ideas to life through this book. Bruce is an editor's editor with a unique ability both to help an author shape his thinking and to make almost any prose sing. I am indebted as well to Steve Ross, who encouraged me to pursue this project when it was the germ of an idea, and to Brian Murray, who makes HarperCollins a welcoming publishing house for any author.

Bob Barnett shepherded this project from its inception to fruition with his always-present enthusiasm and professional approach. I was extremely fortunate to have his wise counsel as this project moved forward.

ACKNOLEDGMENTS

A number of people read early versions of this manuscript, in full or in part. I am indebted to them for unselfishly giving me the benefit of their time and thoughts. They include Elizabeth Stauderman, Eric Rasmussen, Liz Vinogradov, John Wallach, and Lawrence M. Wein. Finally, I would like to thank the women in my life, each of whom contributed to the development of this book in different ways: My wife, Nancy Gayle Judson, who was an unending source of support and encouragement. My daughter, Rebekah Judson, who served as my research assistant for the section in the book dedicated to the collapse of the Soviet Union, and as a general sounding board for my developing ideas. My daughter, Emily Judson, who played a central role in shaping the manuscript by forcing me to explain my thinking in plain English. In particular, her endless stream of questions led me to think particularly hard about cause and effect, and ensured the manuscript was jargon free. Finally, my mother, Betty Judson, who raised me to love books and to believe in their potential to influence our world.

We conclude that the concentration of wealth is natural and inevitable and is periodically alleviated by violent or peaceable partial redistribution. In this view, all economic history is the slow heartbeat of the social organism, a vast systole and diastole of concentrating wealth and compulsive recirculation.

—Will and Ariel Durant, *The Lessons of History*

CONTENTS

THE GATHERING STORM

To the reader: Links to the full text of all of the newspaper and magazine articles excerpted here are posted at the Web site, www.A-E-E.org.

FEARS OVER MISSING NUCLEAR MATERIAL

BBC News, March 7, 2002

"International researchers have warned that the world may be awash in unaccounted weapons-grade uranium and plutonium, after completing a latest database of lost and stolen nuclear material."

A NATION CHALLENGED: SENATE HEARINGS; SOME SEE PANIC AS MAIN EFFECT OF DIRTY BOMBS

New York Times, March 7, 2002

"Radioactive materials in wide use in the United States could be turned into weapons of terror that would probably kill few people but would spread panic and produce severe economic damage, scientists told the Senate Foreign Relations Committee today."

OFFICIAL: ENOUGH MATERIAL MISSING FROM RUSSIA TO BUILD A NUKE

ABC News, February 16, 2005

TESTERS SLIP RADIOACTIVE MATERIALS OVER BORDERS

New York Times, March 28, 2006

THE RISE OF THE SUPER-RICH

New York Times, July 19, 2006

"The new figures show that from 2003 to 2004, the latest year for which there is data, the richest Americans pulled far ahead of everyone else. In the space of that one year, real average income for the top 1 percent of households—those making more than $315,000 in 2004—grew by nearly 17 percent. For the remaining 99 percent, the average gain was less than 3 percent, and that probably makes things look better than they really are, since other data, most notably from the Census Bureau, indicate that the average is bolstered by large gains among the top 20 percent of households. In all, the top 1 percent of households enjoyed 36 percent of all income gains in 2004, on top of an already stunning 30 percent in 2003."

SEIZURES OF "DIRTY BOMB" MATERIALS RISE

United Press International, October 6, 2006

"Such seizures, mostly in Europe, doubled in the past four years . . . there have been more than 300 instances of smugglers caught in such trafficking activities since 2002."

INCOME GAP IS WIDENING, DATA SHOWS

New York Times, March 29, 2007

"Income inequality grew significantly in 2005, with the top 1 percent of Americans—those with incomes that year of more than $348,000—receiving their largest share of national income since 1928, analysis of newly released tax data shows."

DIRTY BOMB WOULD CAUSE PANIC, COST BILLIONS: STUDY

Toronto Star, July 2, 2007

RADIOACTIVE DEVICES DISAPPEARING AT ALARMING RATE

Canadian Television (CTV.ca), July 4, 2007

"Radioactive devices—some of which have the potential to be used in terrorist attacks—have gone missing in alarming numbers in Canada over the past five years.

A new database compiled by The Canadian Press shows that the devices, which are used in everything from medical research to measuring oil wells, are becoming a favoured target of thieves.

At least 76 have gone missing in Canada over the past five years—disappearing from construction sites, specialized tool boxes, and generally growing legs and walking away."

HOMELAND SECURITY OFFICIALS SAY GOVERNMENT UNPREPARED FOR DIRTY BOMB

Congress Daily, November 16, 2007

CONGRESS, ENERGY DEPARTMENT DOCUMENT LOST RADIOACTIVE MATERIAL, TERROR CONCERN

Associated Press, May 5, 2008

"WASHINGTON (AP)—Federal investigators have documented 1,300 cases of lost, stolen or abandoned radioactive material inside the United States over the past five years and have concluded there is a significant risk that terrorists could cobble enough together for a dirty bomb."

RICHEST AMERICANS SEE THEIR INCOME SHARE GROW
Wall Street Journal, July 23, 2008

GEORGIA CHAOS HALTS NUCLEAR SECURITY EFFORT
US was helping track smugglers; Traffickers could take advantage
Boston Globe, August 19, 2008

"WASHINGTON—The chaos in Georgia has forced the United States to halt a high-priority program that was helping the former Soviet republic to identify possible smugglers of nuclear bomb components across its borders, long considered a transit point for terrorists seeking to obtain weapons of mass destruction, according to US officials."

ILO: FINANCIAL CRISIS WILL CAUSE INCOME INEQUALITY GAP TO WIDEN
Voice of America, October 16, 2008

IN WMD REPORT, U.S. GETS A C
Group of Ex-Officials Says Terrorism Threat Remains Real
Washington Post, September 9, 2008

"Seven years after the Sept. 11, 2001, attacks, the federal government has made only limited progress toward preventing a catastrophic nuclear, biological or chemical attack on U.S. soil and combating the proliferation of weapons of mass destruction abroad, according to a report card to be issued tomorrow by 22 former U.S. officials."

U.S. ARMY BRIGADE DEPLOYS FOR HOMELAND MISSION

NationalTerrorAlert.com, September 30, 2008

"For the first time ever, the US military is deploying an active duty regular Army combat unit for full-time use inside the United States to deal with national emergencies, including terrorism, natural disasters and civil unrest."

RATE OF NUCLEAR THEFTS 'DISTURBINGLY HIGH,' MONITORING CHIEF SAYS

New York Times, October 27, 2008

"UNITED NATIONS—Mohamed ElBaradei, the chief of the International Atomic Energy Agency, said in a speech on Monday that the number of reports of nuclear or radioactive material stolen around the world last year was 'disturbingly high.'

Dr. ElBaradei, in his annual report to the General Assembly, said nearly 250 such thefts were reported in the year ending in June.

'The possibility of terrorists obtaining nuclear or other radioactive material remains a grave threat,' he said. 'Equally troubling is the fact that much of this material is not subsequently recovered.' "

REPORT SHOWS STAGNANT UPWARD MOBILITY IN U.S.

Wall Street Journal Real Time Economics Blog, November 12, 2008

"Add it to the other depressing economic news: upward mobility has remained stagnant in the past two decades."

THE FORMERLY MIDDLE CLASS

The New York Times, by David Brooks, November 17, 2008

"This recession will probably have its own social profile. In particular, it's likely to produce a new social group: the formerly middle class. These are people who achieved middle-class status at the tail end of the long boom, and then lost it. To them, the gap between where they are and where they used to be will seem wide and daunting.

These reversals are bound to produce alienation and a political response. If you want to know where the next big social movements will come from, I'd say the formerly middle class."

UNREST CAUSED BY BAD ECONOMY MAY REQUIRE MILITARY ACTION, REPORT SAYS

El Paso Times, December 29, 2008

"EL PASO—A U.S. Army War College report warns an economic crisis in the United States could lead to massive civil unrest and the need to call on the military to restore order."

US REPORT PREDICTS NUCLEAR OR BIOLOGICAL ATTACK BY 2013

Guardian (UK), December 3, 2008

VETERANS A FOCUS OF FBI EXTREMIST PROBE

Wall Street Journal, April 17, 2009

CHAPTER ONE

FREEDOM FROM WANT

To the Reader: This is the only chapter in the book to contain fictional material.

DIRTY BOMB EXPLODES OFF THE COAST OF NEW JERSEY, LIKELY TERRORIST ACTION, PRESIDENT APPEALS FOR CALM

Day 2,* Page 1

"At 3:15 PM yesterday, a radioactive, so-called dirty bomb exploded approximately eight miles off the coast of New Jersey. The bomb is believed to be the work of unnamed terrorists. No one was injured and the winds blew the radioactive cloud out to sea.

At approximately 3:00 PM yesterday, several high-level government offices along with leading newspa-

---

* Note: In this scenario, the first detonation occurs on Day 1. This newspaper report appears the following day.

per and television stations received an unsigned, apparently untraceable e-mail message alerting them to the timing and location of the impending explosion.

The deputy director of the FBI, who appeared live at the press conference along with the director of the FBI and the attorney general, was immediately appointed to lead the investigation of yesterday's events. He stressed 'the primary purpose of a dirty bomb is to incite panic and fear. The actual destructive force is substantially less than the danger associated with conventional weapons.'"

FINANCIAL MARKETS TUMBLE ON LATEST TERRORIST NEWS

Day 2, Page 1

"Stocks tumbled by over 18 percent yesterday on news that a dirty bomb was exploded, most likely by terrorists, off the Atlantic coast of the United States. The Dow fell by 19 percent, the NASDAQ by 21 percent, and the S&P 500 Index by almost 20 percent in one of the largest single-day percentage declines in the history of the stock market.

'The markets abhor uncertainty, and this is one of the most uncertain moments in all of U.S. history,' said the director of equity strategies at Global Funds United. He added, 'No one knows what it means about the ability of business to function in the foreseeable future.'"

SECOND DIRTY BOMB EXPLODES OFF THE COAST OF OREGON, PERPETRATORS STILL UNKNOWN. GOVERNMENT CLOSES FINANCIAL MARKETS

Day 3, Page 1

"Despite heightened security precautions on the nation's shorelines, a second radioactive dirty bomb exploded yesterday off the Pacific coast. Once again, the bomb exploded in an out-of-the-way location and the prevailing winds carried the radioactivity out to sea. No one was injured.

In a repeat of yesterday's events, government and leading news organizations received word of the impending explosion approximately 15 minutes before detonation. Security along both U.S. coasts was increased yesterday, but officials were unable to prevent this latest explosion. It is believed the bomb was planted at least two weeks ago on an obscure buoy used for gathering weather data off the coast of Oregon.

The FBI's deputy director, who is leading the investigation, stated, 'We believe the individuals involved used a remote device to detonate the bomb several weeks after it had been planted.' In discussing the possible motives of those who caused the explosions, he said, 'Our working hypothesis is that these explosions were intended as a demonstration of the capabilities of those involved. It appears they deliberately chose a remote location where no loss of life would occur.'

The president asked the federal agencies responsible for the oversight of U.S. financial markets to close the exchanges until the immediate crisis of uncertainty was resolved. On news of the second bomb's explosion, a panic overwhelmed the stock markets, and the major indices fell, on average, by an additional 17 percent. The Dow, the S&P 500, and the NASDAQ have been devastated since news of the first bomb explosion, and have each now fallen in excess of 35 percent."

"AMERICANS FOR ECONOMIC EQUALITY" TAKE CREDIT FOR RADIOACTIVE BOMBS, WEB SITE FOR PUBLIC COMMUNICATION IS ESTABLISHED

Day 4, Page 1

"The uncertainty that has gripped the nation ended—or at least, transformed to a new stage—at approximately 2:00 PM this afternoon when a group calling itself 'Americans for Economic Equality' sent an e-mail taking credit for the dirty bombs that have exploded off the U.S. coasts.

FBI officials confirmed that they believed the claim to be genuine, as the note included specific information on the types of radioactive material in the two detonated bombs that had not been made public and which only the perpetrators could have known.

The statement reads as follows:

To the American People:

When in the course of human events, it becomes necessary for one people to dissolve the political bands which have connected them with another and to assume among the powers of the earth, the separate and equal station to which the Laws of Nature and of Nature's God entitle them, a decent respect to the opinions of mankind requires that they should declare the causes which impel them to the separation.

America has ceased to be a democracy in all but name. The concentration of power in the hands of a few is nearly total. They run the economy. They control Big Business. Their incomes go up while the rest of us suffer, no matter which party controls Washington. America is now a plutocracy. Our democracy is lost, and must be restored by any means necessary.

We have detonated nuclear explosions off the coasts of the United States. Our intent was not to harm anyone, but to demonstrate that we have the capabilities to wreak havoc if our requests are not acted upon.

We believe that it is the rightful role of government to ensure that every citizen has a fair shot at realizing the American Dream. If the federal government had not abandoned this role, we would not be issuing this statement today. Our national government no longer serves the interests of all Americans.

Freedom from Want is a basic human right. Governments throughout history have oppressed their people, and suffered for it. America's government has ceased to work for its people, and must suffer the consequences. We will not stop until we have a government that works for the many, not the few. The many have the right to:

- Free education, at all levels
- Their own home, free from vulture banks
- Free healthcare for all

These basic needs are the only means to ensure Freedom from Want. When the education system favors the rich over the rest, it is not democratic. When millions of hardworking Americans lose their homes, our democracy has failed. When our health system favors the rich over the rest, it is not democratic.

Unfortunately, we see no way to accomplish our objectives without making the following threat: If our demands are not met within 45 days, we will set off a series of dirty bombs in American cities.

We have established a Web site, www.A-E-E.org, which we will use should it be necessary to communicate with you and the public in the future. If access to this site is in any way limited by the government, we will instantly detonate the pre-planted bombs. At this site, we invite Americans to review the information we have assembled, and to discuss concerns about their economic security.

We don't doubt that your police forces will spend untold hours looking for us. We are no longer here. Many bombs are planted throughout the nation, and we can activate them remotely.

After the reforms we have requested are instituted, we pledge to the American people that we will reveal the locations of all of the dirty bombs planted on the U.S. mainland, so they can be peacefully removed.

Sincerely,
Americans for Economic Equality

I am not for the return of that definition of liberty under which for many years a free people were being gradually regimented into the service of a privileged few.
—Franklin Roosevelt

PRESIDENT RESPONDS TO TERRORISTS
Day 4, Page 1

"The president, who remained at an undisclosed location, responded to the terrorists by issuing a brief statement that read, 'It has always been and will always be the policy of this government not to negotiate with terrorists. We cannot exist as a democratic nation if we allow anyone else to dictate our laws to us.'

The secretary of Homeland Security, who spoke with reporters, indicated that he had no reason to believe the terrorists were anything other than a domestic organization. 'There are no indications that a foreign power or transnational organization lie behind them,' he said."

PRESIDENT RETURNS TO WASHINGTON, WILL SPEAK TO CONGRESS AND THE NATION

Day 6, Page 1

"The president returned to the White House yesterday, amidst a heavy guard. As part of a pre-arranged plan, the vice president left the Capitol for an undisclosed location.

A senior White House spokesman announced that the president would appear before a Joint Session of Congress to discuss his plans for dealing with the new terrorist threat."

AN ANGRY AND DIVIDED NATION LOOKS INWARD

Day 7, Page 1

"As the public anticipates the president's speech, the mood of the nation is angry and divided.

Historically, when America is attacked the nation rallies around the president and symbols of national unity. In contrast, this latest terrorist threat seems to have led to a mix of reactions. They range from shell-shocked, to angry, to introspective.

Of course, not a single serious commentator could be found who had any sympathy for the terrorists' methods. Yet there are hints of understanding in addition to the outrage. The executive director of Americans to Eliminate Poverty, a Washington think tank, said, 'Tens of millions of Americans exist in lives of quiet desperation, wondering how they will have enough to eat next week. Is it any wonder that someone has finally lashed out, albeit in this despicable manner?'

Meanwhile, most commentators expressed almost entirely opposite views, "Right now, I think it's incumbent on all of us to support the lawful, democratically empowered government of the United States,' said the director of the conservative Washington-based Alliance for Progress. 'At this moment, what the terrorists most want is to divide our nation and create sympathy for their cause,' he added. 'This is the time for one thing and one thing only: to ensure that our basic way of life and economy is not destroyed.'"

GOVERNMENT AGENCIES UNDERTAKE MASSIVE SEARCHES FOR HIDDEN DIRTY BOMBS

Day 8, Page 1

"The FBI, the Department of Homeland Security, and state and local officials are undertaking a furious hunt for any information related to dirty bombs that might be hidden on U.S. territory. Several law enforcement agencies are looking into any possible leads associated with the identity of the terrorists.

The terrorists claim that the bombs are already planted on American soil. To evade detection the radiation signature associated with the bombs is probably shielded from even the most sophisticated equipment. Experts say this could be achieved with casings made of lead, among other possibilities. Sources within several law-enforcement agencies write that many American cities are already equipped with sophisticated radiation-detection equipment, yet no alarms have been triggered. The most likely means of finding the bombs is to find the terrorists themselves."

PRESIDENT ASKS CONGRESS FOR DECLARATION OF WAR ON TERRORISTS. FIRST REQUEST TO CONGRESS SINCE 1941

Day 9, Page 1

"Last night, in an unprecedented request, the president asked a joint session of Congress to declare war, as prescribed by the Constitution, on the terrorist organization that calls itself Americans for Economic Equality. This is the first formal request by a president for a declaration of war since 1941, when Franklin Roosevelt asked Congress to declare war on Nazi Germany.

TEXT OF THE PRESIDENT'S SPEECH
TO CONGRESS AND THE NATION:

Mr. Speaker, members of the Senate, members of the House, and ladies and gentlemen in this hall and throughout the nation, thank you for meeting with me here tonight.

As you all know, our country has been the subject of two recent nuclear attacks from a terrorist group. While there was no loss of life, this represented a milestone that I am sad to say occurred during my presidency: the first hostile explosions of nuclear devices on American territory by enemies of the United States.

Now, I would like to tell you what I can, without compromising our ongoing investigation.

To the best of our knowledge, these enriched uranium bombs were planted by a radical fringe group of disaffected Americans. All of our international contacts and intelligence agencies feel confident this is not a plot inspired by a foreign government to destabilize the United States.

We are in the process of attempting to determine the source of the enriched uranium used in these bombs. This should provide us both with clues as to the names of the perpetrators of this despicable act, and give us some indication of how much uranium the terrorists have actually gathered.

The bombs were low-powered dirty nuclear devices. This means that they could not, under any circumstances, have set off a nuclear chain reaction. I would like to stress that these devices had less explosive power than many conventional bombs. The primary purpose of dirty bombs of this type is to create panic and sow economic havoc. If we remain united, then neither panic nor economic disarray needs to happen here.

The full range of components needed to carry out the

terrorists' plans requires a sophisticated knowledge of nuclear devices and electronics. Our federal agencies have begun the task of seeking to identify individuals with the necessary credentials, and a radical history, who might have been involved in these attacks.

That is what we know at this time. As more information becomes available, we will make every effort to keep you as apprised as possible.

Now, I have come to a discussion of perhaps the most difficult decision I have had to make as president. The terrorists have given us a timetable, which we must assume is real. As a consequence, we have a very limited amount of time to find an unknown enemy, and all of their weapons.

I will do whatever is necessary to ensure the protection of our freedom. As a nation, we have been attacked. I am appearing before you tonight to formally ask for a declaration of war against the terrorist group that calls itself Americans for Economic Equality. The attorney general has provided me with an opinion that it is appropriate for Congress to declare war against a group of individuals that has attacked this country with weapons as powerful as those possessed by sovereign nations.

We must let our enemies know that in the face of an imminent threat, we will use every power at our disposal to track down and eliminate threats to our physical security and economic well-being.

At this hour in which our liberty is tested, I feel compelled to remind you of the words of a great American patriot, John F. Kennedy, who died in the service of his country. In his inaugural address Kennedy said, 'Let every nation know, whether it wishes us well or ill, that we shall pay any price, bear any burden, meet any hardship, support any friend or oppose any foe to assure the survival and the success of liberty.' I trust that through the actions of Congress in the coming days, we will send this same message to those who threaten our liberty.

I am confident that with the help of this Congress, the support of the American people, and with the blessings of God, we will continue to enjoy the fruits of liberty and opportunity that have long been the hallmark of this extraordinary nation.

Thank you. God bless America and good night."

CONGRESS GRANTS PRESIDENT DECLARATION OF WAR BY WIDE MAJORITY IN BOTH HOUSES. ATTORNEY GENERAL PROVIDES WRITTEN GUARANTEES ON CIVIL LIBERTIES

Day 10, Page 1

SECRETARY OF HOMELAND SECURITY ANNOUNCES GOVERNMENT WILL NOT INTERFERE WITH TERRORIST WEB SITE

Day 12, Page 1

TELEVISION INTERVIEW WITH SENATOR LOUIS ROBERTS

Day 13, 8:00 PM

"INTERVIEWER: Joining me tonight is the senior senator from Minnesota, Louis Roberts. Senator Roberts is one of the few members of Congress to vote against the Declaration of War requested by the president in response to the unprecedented terrorist threat.

Senator Roberts, thank you for coming tonight. I see that you arrived tonight in a military vehicle. Can you please tell our audience why you voted against the president's Declaration of War?

SENATOR ROBERTS: Thank you, I appreciate this opportunity to speak directly to the American people.

As I hope every American knows, I have dedicated my professional career and my entire life to working to build a greater America. I absolutely abhor the tactics used by the terrorists. They are not freedom fighters, and they are certainly not patriots.

Their abhorrent tactics have, however, focused attention on a fundamental problem in our society: the extreme and growing economic inequality that divides America's most fortunate and least fortunate citizens. In numerous pieces of proposed legislation, I am already on record as favoring policies that will provide for universal healthcare, create a more equitable tax system, and create a more equitable sharing of the benefits of this country's extraordinary productivity.

It seems to me that, without negotiating or giving in to terrorist demands, we still have the opportunity right now to discuss what's best for America. Before this crisis, polls showed that over 80 percent of the American public did not believe the government acts in their best interest, and that over 50 percent of the population is struggling or suffering. For the first time, over half the nation believes children will have a less prosperous life than their parents had.

These statistics do not justify threats of violence, but they may help explain it. We face an unprecedented loss of faith in the American Dream. I believe all of these sad statistics reflect, at least in part, the growth of extreme economic inequality in America. Right now, America has the highest economic inequality of any industrialized nation, and by some measures the highest economic inequality in our entire history. Once we rush to war it will become almost impossible for us to have a reasoned discussion of the critical issues that helped inspire the conflict in the first place.

INTERVIEWER: Senator, do you intend to use the current crisis to push your agenda, even if it coincides to some degree with the terrorists'?

SENATOR ROBERTS: I am first and foremost a patriot

and a supporter of the Constitution. The Congress of the United States has voted to go to war, and I will do everything in my power to support our war efforts in this time of crisis.

I absolutely abhor the actions of these terrorists, who have wreaked enormous physical and environmental damage, and hurt the very people they claim they want to help. My goal is first and foremost to stop these terrible acts and bring the terrorists to justice. I believe the way to help the most unfortunate is to create a more just society through our legislative process."

TERRORIST WEB SITE WARNS THAT "LOW-LEVEL RADIATION BOMB" WILL EXPLODE IN OFFICES OF COUNTRYONE BANK IN 30 MINUTES. ENCOURAGES IMMEDIATE EVACUATION

Breaking News: Day 15, 10:30 AM, broadcast television report

"**ANCHOR:** This is James McSweeney the anchor of California's independent television news channel. We have just learned that the terrorist group calling itself Americans for Economic Equality has warned, through its Web site, that a dirty bomb will explode in the next half hour in or near the headquarters of CountryOne Bank in Calabasas, California.

The terrorist group has posted a warning stating that 'To further demonstrate our capacity to explode dirty bombs on the mainland United States, we will detonate a low-level radiation bomb outside or in the area of the headquarters of CountryOne Bank in Calabasas, California, at 11:00 AM today. CountryOne's vampire loans have put over 100,000 families on the street. To prevent loss of life, we urge that all citizens within the surrounding five blocks be evacuated.'

State and local officials are rushing to evacuate the ten blocks surrounding the CountryOne offices, an area larger than the evacuation zone identified by the terrorists.

State and federal officials say that there is insufficient time to evacuate the area and search for a shielded bomb with sophisticated radiation detectors."

COUNTRYONE OFFICES EXPLODE IN DIRTY BOMB EXPLOSION

Breaking News: Day 15, 11:05 AM, broadcast television report

"ANCHOR: The terrorist group has carried out its threat to explode the first-ever dirty bomb on the U.S. mainland. We have just learned that a low-level radiation bomb exploded at the headquarters of CountryOne Bank at approximately 11:00 AM this morning. Because the offices had been evacuated, there was no loss of life. The damage to the building was substantial and officials have indicated that a clean-up of all radioactive materials will take place.

The reaction around the country was one of widespread panic. The terrorists claim to have hidden many more dirty bombs, and Americans in many locations are confronting the possibility that their neighborhoods could be contaminated by radiation, or worse."

TERRORIST WEB SITE SEES 15 MILLION VISITORS SINCE COUNTRYONE ATTACK

Part One of a Two-Part Series

Day 18, Page 1

"With the recent attack at CountryOne's headquarters, public attention has shifted to the terrorist Web site at www.A-E-E.org. In the two days since the explosion of the dirty bomb in California, over fifteen million Americans are estimated to have visited the site.

The site, hosted by American Hosting Inc., is prepaid for two years and was established using a trail of false names and bank checks that appear to make its owners untraceable.

Using the appropriate password, the terrorists have the ability to post new information at the site at any time from any location in the world, making it effectively impossible to trace their identity."

CONTENT OF TERRORIST WEB SITE SHOCKS, SURPRISES, AND SEDUCES. ALL AMERICANS INVITED TO POST THEIR VIEWS

Part Two of a Two-Part Series

Day 19, Page 1

"For most Americans, the first visit to the now highly trafficked Web site of the Americans for Economic Equality (www.A-E-E.org) is a surprise. Instead of anger and vitriol, visitors are treated to links and excerpts from mainstream newspapers and magazines, such as the *Wall Street Journal, BusinessWeek,* the *New York Times,* the *Washington Post,* and similar publications, which document the growing economic inequality in the United States, and the increasing economic plight of the middle class and working Americans.

The A-E-E.org site is divided into several distinct sections, including:

- A warnings area that includes the terrorists' letter setting out the group's demands. This is the area where the group posted the warning of the CountryOne attack before the bomb exploded.

- An American inequality area that provides links, headlines, and excerpts from hundreds of articles that originally appeared in mainstream newspapers, magazines, scholarly works, and government publications, that demonstrate how economic inequality has risen to historic levels in the United States, and detail the potentially negative impact of this trend.

- A forums area where individual Americans can post their thoughts on a variety of questions related to economic inequality, such as: Do you believe your children will have a better life than you? Do you believe that you can achieve the American Dream? and Is America a society of haves and have nots?

- An opinions section that allows individual visitors to participate in polls on a wide range of issues associated with economic inequality. After each visitor's vote, updated results are instantly displayed. Some of the questions Americans have been answering include: Are you satisfied with the schools available to your family? Do you have adequate healthcare? Can you afford to retire? Are you able to afford a college education for your children? In your opinion, is the American tax system fair?

- An online petition requesting the signatures of the American people. The petition, in part, asks 'The president and the Congress of the United States to provide all Americans with free healthcare, a free college education, and affordable housing.'

Several thousand people have posted comments on the terrorist site in the past week. While many people have used these forums, which are not moderated, to excoriate the terrorists, others display a deep frustration with the state of their economic lives and place blame for these frustrations partly on the shoulders of the government."

SENATORS BOB KING AND LOUIS ROBERTS INTRODUCE LEGISLATION PROMOTING TERRORIST AGENDA

Day 24, Page 1

"In a joint statement issued yesterday, Republican senator Bob King of Nevada and Democratic senator Louis Roberts of Minnesota said, 'Those who seek to make this nation a better place for everyone, as opposed to a privileged few, have long supported improving the quality of life for all Americans. No sane American supports the terrorists' methods, yet our nation cannot shut its eyes to the underlying conditions that have led to this despicable behavior.

'We have drafted and introduced a bill that addresses the deprivation in healthcare, education, and housing many of our citizens experience as a result of extreme economic inequality in America. We believe that the estimated cost to the nation of implementing these reforms in the short-run will be far exceeded by the long-run benefits of creating a better educated, healthier, more productive citizenry that can meet the global challenges needed for the twenty-first-century workforce.'"

SENATE DECISIVELY REJECTS BY A VOTE OF 93 TO 7 LEGISLATION PROPOSED BY KING AND ROBERTS

Day 27, Page 1

A DIVIDED HOUSE CANNOT STAND

By Brian Jenkins, author of The Danger of Extreme Economic Inequality

Day 29, Op-Ed Page

"It is a testament to the greatness of America that at a time of war I am free to write this article.

America is the one nation conceived on an ideal. Unlike the majority of nations, which are accidents of geography and language, we were founded on the principles of freedom, democracy, and equality. For the majority of our history, we have lived up to this noble beginning and served as a beacon of light to oppressed peoples throughout the world. The vast numbers of immigrants have always served as a clear demonstration that the world did indeed perceive this nation as the land of opportunity.

Unfortunately, somewhere in the past half century we lost our way. In other contexts, I have written about why I believe our path diverged from a strengthening of opportunity to a weakening of the ability for every hardworking citizen to realize the American Dream. These reasons do not matter today. What does matter is that the recent terrorist actions have further exposed the deep and unsustainable nature of our society.

By some measures, we are at the highest levels of economic inequality in the recorded history of the Republic. While a privileged few lead lives of great wealth, the average American family has debts equal to far more than its annual income. Over the past decade, economic insecurity and the decline of our formerly vibrant middle class have become the norm, rather than the exception. Now, joblessness has reached its highest level in a generation.

The president, a long-time advocate of social reform, is squandering a unique opportunity to reshape society in a way that will put us back on track with the ideals that represent the best of America. The alternative, if we survive this crisis without an economy or nation in ruins, is the continuation of a sharply divided polity—where the mass of the citizenry feels more and more like it exists under the yoke of the privileged few.

With the first dirty bomb attack, the government understandably anticipated that, as happened in the aftermath of 9/11, the nation would unify and resolutely face whatever the crisis might bring. Unfortunately, the parallel with 9/11 was a poor one. The World Trade Center attack was an attack on all of us. In contrast, the terrorist threat has given voice to the previously disregarded feelings of many Americans. These Americans wonder if anyone cares about them, and consider the idea of real equal opportunity a false promise.

Military historians will say that there is one fundamental rule of warfare: Divided societies rarely win. I urge the president and Congress to consider whether this is an opportunity to right a long-festering wrong. There is no one, myself most of all, who condones the form of action chosen by the terrorists. Yet polls consistently show that the vast majority of Americans do support the goals of greater equality in access to healthcare, education, and affordable housing, but certainly not the chosen means of the AEE. I do not believe that acting to create a just, more equitable society will diminish the freedom of our nation. If ever there was a moment for pragmatism in place of principle it is now."

ANGER BUILDING IN AMERICA, DIRECTED AT FEDERAL GOVERNMENT

Day 30, Page 1

"A strong undercurrent of anger is building in working America. The anger is focused not at the terrorists, who have brought the U.S. economy to a practical standstill, and now threaten an unknown number of lives, but at the federal government, which seems powerless to stop them.

Polls indicate that over 80 percent of Americans are angry because they believe 'the government has not kept me safe.' 'The fundamental responsibility of any government is first and foremost to keep the people safe from physical harm,' said Ronald Levine, a professor of constitutional law at Harvard Law School. 'Once a government fails this test, it can lose its legitimacy.' "

FURIOUS SEARCH FOR DIRTY BOMBS CONTINUES
Day 31, Page 1

"Over the past month, every train and bus station, every major public monument, and entire city blocks have been swept for signs of radiation. Hundreds of thousands of Dumpsters have been physically examined. Sophisticated technology has been used to search for signs of freshly dug ground. Yet experts say the search is impossibly difficult. A shielded dirty bomb could be easily hidden and placed in any innocent-looking container."

TERRORISTS WARN OF DIRTY BOMB EXPLOSION IN BIRMINGHAM, AL, AT HEADQUARTERS OF NATIONAL CORRECTIONS INC., NATION'S LARGEST PRIVATE PRISON OPERATOR. BOMB SET TO EXPLODE IN 30 MINUTES
Breaking News: Day 32, 11:00 AM, broadcast television report

TERRORISTS DETONATE DIRTY BOMB AT NCI HEADQUARTERS IN BIRMINGHAM. NO REPORTED INJURIES. EXPERTS SAY AREA WILL BE UNINHABITABLE FOR YEARS

Breaking News: Day 32, 11:35 AM, broadcast television report

PANIC SURGES THROUGHOUT THE NATION

Day 33, Page 1

DO THE RIGHT THING

Editorial by Paul Krug

Day 35, Op-Ed Page

"Americans are angry, and it's not hard to understand why. Over the past month, what should have been a deadly serious effort to save a nation on the brink of full-scale panic, and an economy in desperate straits, turned, instead, into a display of grand incompetence.

Our government has demonstrated that it is powerless to stop a looming calamity of inestimable proportions. The president keeps repeating that he will not negotiate with terrorists, there is no evidence of any progress by the nation's many security services, and everyone refuses to even consider that the societal problems identified by the terrorist crisis are real.

Somehow, Washington has lost any sense of

what's at stake—of the reality that we may well be falling into an abyss of chaos, panic, and economic ruin, and that if we do, it will be very hard to get out again.

The credit markets have seized up in a way that makes the fall 2008 credit crunch look like a walk in the park. As everyone from banks to consumers hoards cash (or gold if they can find it), all but the most essential spending has ceased. At this moment, economic carnage is the only way to describe the state of the United States. Trillions of dollars in pension assets have been wiped out as the stock and bond markets have reacted to the terrorist crisis. Americans have seen the value of their homes and the value of their investments plummet. It's only a matter of time before we incur massive job losses as well.

People are frightened. They fear for their physical safety and the possibility that they might need to permanently abandon their homes at a moment's notice should the terrorists explode a dirty bomb in their area. As the crisis has unfolded, there is the pervading sense that the American way of life as we have known it for over 200 years has been irreparably damaged. People wonder whether they will ever feel safe again.

Most of all, Americans feel betrayed by their government. After years of warnings, years of rhetoric, and years of investment in homeland security, the government was unable to prevent this most obvious and basic threat to national security.

We are now a divided nation. Violent protests have erupted across the nation. Citizens are angrily urging the government to reconsider its stance. So far, their protests have fallen on deaf ears.

There is a solution for the president that does not involve negotiating with the terrorists, and that is to do the right thing. For years, we have known that our healthcare system and our education system are travesties. They have failed to serve the needs of a large section of our society. At the same time, millions of Americans have been losing their homes. Now, America has been called to account.

The president and his administration should take this crisis as a once-in-a-lifetime opportunity to fix America. There is no shame in establishing a decent healthcare or educational system. It's something we all know we should have done long ago.

Let's not let pride go before the fall."

IN MEETING WITH PRESIDENT, STATE GOVERNORS WARN FUTURE OF THE NATION MAY BE AT STAKE

Day 36, Page 1

"The president assembled a meeting of the nation's governors to convey a series of warnings about what the nation could expect. Instead, he was apparently shocked to receive serious warnings of a different kind from the attending governors. In no mood for a briefing, a number of governors expressed their frustration with the administration's inability to keep people safe.

The meeting was held without the presence of the governors' aides or press, but administration sources reported that the discussion quickly took on an angry tone. One after another, individual governors told the president that if he could not guarantee the safety of the citizens of their states then the governors might be forced to act on their own. One governor who refused to be identified by name told this reporter, 'I was elected first and foremost to keep the people of my state physically safe. If the federal government can't do its job, then I need to do mine.'"

MILLIONS OF ANGRY PROTESTERS GATHER ACROSS THE NATION. DESPITE VIOLENCE, ARMY DOES NOT FIRE ON U.S. CITIZENS

Day 37, Page 1

"Millions of Americans took to the streets today to protest the government's handling of the terrorist crisis.

As violence flared across the country, military personnel were confronted with their worst nightmare: Do they fire on the very citizens they have sworn to protect?

The answer was a resounding No.

The Pentagon acknowledged tonight that the president had issued secret orders not to fire on U.S. civilians. According to the secret presidential directive, deadly force was not to be employed 'except in the most extreme and violent situations threatening the lives of innocent citizens.'

One of the largest protests took place in Washington, D.C., where several hundred thousand people were reported to have gathered on the Mall outside the Capitol."

TERRORISTS THREATEN FLORIDA CITIES, PANIC ENSUES

Day 38, Page 1

"Less than a week after exploding a dirty bomb in Birmingham, the Americans for Economic Equality have announced a new, more menacing threat via their Web site at www.A-E-E.org: If the United States does not meet the group's demands, a high-power dirty bomb will explode within 48 hours in one of Florida's largest cities: Miami, Orlando, Jacksonville, Tampa, or St. Petersburg.

This latest threat represents a new, more frightening turn of events in America's war with the AEE. To date, the group has threatened only specific sites, and provided ample opportunity for citizens to evacuate. Now, the resources of Florida and the nation are stretched—and perhaps unable to meet the shorter deadline and far larger evacuation required.

In a panic, residents of all five cities jammed the roads, bringing traffic to a virtual standstill.

Governor James Wilde has called the Florida legislature into emergency session in Tallahassee."

FLORIDA SECEDES

Day 39, Page 1

The governor of Florida announced today that Florida was withdrawing from the United States of America, declaring its own sovereignty, planning to fashion a sovereign nation, and calling for the return of all Florida national guard units to its borders under the command of the Florida governor—as opposed to the U.S. federal government. The stunning announcement was made by Florida governor James Wilde after meeting in a seven-hour closed-door joint session of both houses of the Florida state legislature.

Faced with panicked citizens jamming the highways from the state's largest cities, rising anarchy, growing violence, an economy on the brink of ruin, and the perception of an intransigent but powerless federal government, the governor and the legislature of Florida shocked the nation by announcing the state's withdrawal from the Union. In a prepared statement, the governor announced that what he called a sovereign nation will now provide universal healthcare and free tuition at state universities to all residents. A Florida commission to reform laws governing foreclosures and homeowner rights has also been established.

The unexpected news, occurring as the terrorist crisis escalated, was so shocking that federal officials were unwilling to publicly comment on the action. One high-placed official who would make a statement only on the condition of anonymity said, 'Florida's action is clearly illegal, and I can't believe they gave in to terrorists. But who is going to publicly condemn a state government for protecting its people and economy when the federal government can't or won't?'

With almost no exceptions, Florida national guard units were already within the state. As these units left U.S. federal facilities, no attempts were made by the U.S. military to prevent their withdrawal. Sources report that permitting this nonviolent troop movement reflected a direct order that originated with the U.S. president.

In a brief statement, Governor Wilde commented, 'I have sworn an oath to protect the citizens of Florida. The government of the United States has clearly failed in its responsibility to protect us. It is wrong for any terrorist group to target Florida's citizens over a dispute with the government of the United States. We have decided that we must now act to protect and provide for ourselves.'

The Web site of the Americans for Economic

Equality immediately posted a statement withdrawing the threat to Florida's cities. Reaction was vociferous around the country. Many commentators excoriated the government of Florida for abandoning the United States in its hour of need."

NEW YORK AND ILLINOIS JOIN FLORIDA IN DECLARING INDEPENDENCE. OTHER STATES EXPECTED TO FOLLOW

Day 49, Page 1

"The crisis in the governance of the nation—if it is to remain one nation—deepened yesterday, as the governors of New York and Illinois declared their states to be independent. The announcements were generally believed to be an effort by the state governments to protect their citizens from targeting by the Americans for Economic Equality."

PRESIDENT RESIGNS, ASKS PEOPLE TO CALL NEW CONSTITUTIONAL CONVENTION

Day 51, Page 1

"Last night, appearing at an emergency joint session of Congress scheduled earlier in the day, the president resigned in favor of the vice president, called on the former states to send representatives to a new Constitutional Convention to be scheduled in 45 days in Philadelphia, and told the country that it would be far stronger united by a common heritage than divided by fear. The full text of the president's speech appears below:

Mr. Speaker, Mr. Vice President, my countrymen. I come before you tonight at a time of great national peril. For the second time in our history as a people, we have divided into separate nations, and our future as one people is in jeopardy.

At the conclusion of this evening, I will, in accordance with federal law, tender my written resignation to the secretary of state. Our vice president, who has served this country so well—as vice president and previously as majority leader of the Senate, and a senator for over 20 years—will then replace me as the leader of our country, which remains the greatest nation on earth.

Throughout my tenure as president, and throughout the terrorist crisis, I have done my best to protect this nation, and to live up to the oath I swore on entering office to defend our Constitution. Unfortunately, recent events have led me to conclude that I have ultimately failed in maintaining the liberty and prosperity of our nation. Each night I ask myself what I could have done differently. Harry Truman is famous for saying 'The buck stops here,' and the ultimate responsibility for the depth of the crisis we face is mine. I believe the severity of the crisis, my own exhaustion, and the need for someone new who will inspire your confidence require that I step down.

I was brought up to revere our Constitution. Many Americans don't realize that on entering office my oath is associated with the Constitution and not the national prosperity. As president I promised that I would, and I quote, 'to the best of my ability, preserve, protect and defend the Constitution of the United States.' My oath was to preserve our form of republican government—which the founders of our nation viewed as ultimately the most significant task of any president.

It may be that a document and system of government created for a fledgling eighteenth-century group of disparate Colonies cannot adequately serve a great twenty-first-century nation. But before our states go their separate ways, I plead with you and the leaders of each state to give unity one more opportunity. As my last official act, I am therefore issuing a proclamation in which I appeal to all of the existing and former states of the United States of America to send representatives to a new Constitutional Convention, which will meet in 45 days. I ask that the convention meet not in Washington, D.C., but in Philadelphia, where our first Constitution was drafted over 200 years ago.

Our existing Constitution provides several provisions for how a new Constitutional Convention might be called, which involve the Congress or requests from the state legislatures. To put it simply, if two-thirds of the states send representatives to this gathering, then it will be a valid Constitutional Convention.

My fellow countrymen, this has been a very difficult and trying time for our land. Many of you have suffered terrible economic dislocations as a result of recent events. Our national wealth, as measured in dollars and cents, has been severely eroded. However, the great wealth of America has always resided not in pieces of paper but in the spirit, ingenuity, and determination of our people. I beg you not to forget that or to lose sight of the great strength that is the idea of America in the days ahead. *We are far stronger united by our common heritage than divided by fear.*

If we can find a way to once more come together—on terms that ensure a larger stake in our society for all Americans—I have every confidence that we will once again be the greatest nation on earth. As a result of our trial, we will also be that much closer to the ideals of Thomas Jefferson, when he wrote the immortal words in our Declaration of Independence, 'We hold these truths to be self-evident: That all men are created equal; that they are endowed by their Creator with certain unalienable Rights; that among these are Life, Liberty and the pursuit of Happiness.' Perhaps this division of our nation will, like the trial of the Civil War, result in a new meaning of the word equality as we apply it to all Americans.

It has been the greatest honor of my life to serve as the president of the greatest nation on earth. I am certain that we will once more be a confident and prosperous nation. May God bless you and good night.

CHAPTER TWO

IMMUNITY FROM HISTORY?

The possibility of a second revolution in the United States (or third, if you include the secession of the Southern states in 1861) is generally accorded almost no serious consideration by scholars or policymakers. If it is raised at all, it is typically discarded because of the difficulty associated with organizing a coordinated uprising, and the self-correcting nature of our democracy. America has managed peaceful transfers of power for over two centuries—with the important exception of the Civil War. Yet revolutions do happen, and often with little warning. The fall of the Soviet Union—the world's only other superpower in the late twentieth century—happened quickly and without prior warning. One day President Reagan called the Soviet Union "an evil empire," and the next day that nation imploded, after a series of cascading, uncoordinated events.

This book is not intended as a prediction so much

as a warning. Economic inequality is the single greatest predictor of revolution, and inequality in America has reached catastrophic levels. As extreme economic inequality increasingly divides the country, the nation becomes far more vulnerable to the disruptive forces that could be unleashed by a single, highly divisive event. The preceding scenario focused on terrorism. Yet, once the fabric of a society is flammable there are any number of ways to ignite it. Perhaps riots after several million foreclosures. Perhaps a natural disaster. The preceding chapter's fiction could have used a wide range of scenarios based on activities by the extreme right or extreme left of the political spectrum, as well as any number of severe accidents or catastrophic occurrences (either natural or man-made). A healthy society can withstand severe shocks. The question is, are we fundamentally a healthy society? History teaches that there are limits to the extent of acceptable economic inequality in any society. We have moved beyond these limits. The glue that holds our society together is weakened. Perhaps the body politic is not so different from the human body: When our immune system is working properly our resistance is high, and we can fight off any number of potentially life-threatening illnesses. But when we have already suffered internal injuries, our ability to effectively battle a contagion is far weaker.

Recently, the United States marked a largely unrecognized milestone: *Economic inequality in the nation is now at its highest level since the availability of accurate records in the* *early 1900s.*[*] The top earning 10 percent of U.S. families receive 49.3 percent of all U.S. household income, including capital gains. By comparison, this top 10 percent received a substantially lower 34.2 percent of the nation's total household income in 1979.[†] The comparison is far starker for the super-rich, the top 1 percent.

The bulk of the explosion of inequality has occurred in the past 30 years, and it shows no sign of lessening. In 1979 the top 1 percent of Americans received 10 percent of the nation's total income, by 2006 this figure had more than doubled, to over 22.8 percent.[†] The top 1 percent of American families now take home one-quarter to one-fifth of all of the household income generated by society.

Writing in December 2007, Nobel Prize–winning economist Joseph Stiglitz concluded, "A rising tide lifted all yachts. Inequality in America is now widening at a rate not seen in three-quarters of a century. A young male in his 30s today

---

[*]   Accurate records related to the distribution of income in the United States have been available for the period since 1913, when the modern federal income tax system was introduced. As discussed in chapter four, there are a variety of ways to measure income inequality. The measure used to indicate this "milestone" of inequality is the income of the top 10 percent of all U.S. families as a percentage of total U.S. income. In 2006 this threshold exceeded, by a small margin, the previous high set in 1928.

[†]   These statistics reflect results for 2006, which is the most recent data analyzed as this book goes to press. Incomes include capital gains. Data compiled by Professor Emmanuel Saez, Department of Economics, University of California, Berkeley, and available at http://elsa.berkeley.edu/~saez/TabFig2006prel.xls (updated July 2008). This data is analyzed in Emmanuel Saez, "Striking It Richer: The Evolution of Top Incomes in the United States (updated using 2006 preliminary estimates)," working paper, March 15, 2008. This paper can be downloaded from Professor Saez's Web page at http://elsa.berkeley.edu/~saez/.

[‡]   Ibid.

has an income, adjusted for inflation, that is 12 percent less than what his father was making 30 years ago . . . America's class structure may not have arrived there yet, but it's heading in the direction of Brazil's and Mexico's."[*]

If we were to plot out U.S. economic inequality since 1913 on a graph, it would essentially look like the letter U—with inequality peaking in the 1928–29 period, descending and forming a trough from the late 1950s to the 1970s, and then accelerating back upward starting in the late 1970s. In effect, the 1960s and 1970s, were the golden age of economic equality in the United States. (I am speaking only of economics, not social equality.) For example, the top 1 percent of all American households received approximately 18 percent of the nation's income in 1913. This total peaked at 23.9 percent in 1928, declined rapidly to 11.3 percent in 1944—forming the left side of the U—and continued to decline at a slower rate until 1976 to 8.9 percent. Then began a steep upward ascent in 1979, forming the right side of the U. As noted above, by 2006, the top 1 percent of American households had increased to over 22.8 percent of all household income.[†] While the data for 2007 is not yet available, the likelihood is that this total will exceed 1928 as an all-time high.

This U shape can be seen whether one looks at the income share of the top 10 percent, 5 percent, or 1 per-

---

[*]   Joseph Stiglitz, "The Economic Consequences of Mr. Bush," *Vanity Fair*, December 2007.

[†]   Saez, "Striking It Richer."

cent of all earners. However, the driving factor behind all three U-shaped graphs is the top 1 percent. Truly, we have become an economic oligopoly. Is it an accident that the peaks of the U occurred just before the crashes of 1929 and 2008? Surely not. Economists have not focused on it, but a strong argument can be made that rising inequality directly contributed to both catastrophic crashes.

Extreme economic inequality ultimately leads to political instability and often revolution. One scholar of comparative politics, surveying the literature on the subject, puts it like this: "Among contemporary political scientists it has become axiomatic that material inequality and political instability go together."[*] Yet virtually everyone who has studied the dangerous impact of extreme economic inequality on a wide variety of societies has effectively concluded that America is immune to the potentially disruptive effects of extreme inequality. Even authors of political thrillers, who have created scenarios for coups and revolutions based on terrorism, assassinations, and enemy conspiracies, have avoided homegrown unrest: it just isn't possible. The idea is effectively taboo in our society. We take it as an unalterable given that our constitutional system of governance, as supported by the people, is everlasting.

My contention is that unchecked and rising economic inequality is an indicator of a dysfunctional democracy that is spiraling downward. A careful historical analysis suggests

---

[*]   John Rapley, *Globalization and Inequality: Neoliberalism's Downward Spiral* (Lynne Rienner, 2004), 1.

such societies inevitably fall prey to internal collapse through conflict or corruption.[*] The threat is real and increasing.

The argument that the United States may face political instability in the near future undoubtedly seems far-fetched. However, in late 2007, it was similarly inconceivable that by early 2009 the world would lose 40 percent of its wealth,[†] the United States; financial system would be in chaos, and the country (as well as the rest of the world) would be facing the most desperate economic climate since the Great Depression. A few Cassandras were disregarded as they predicted a crisis largely on the basis that economic history indicated the financial system was not sustainable. Whenever our society moves beyond boundaries of balance and stability, the potential for untold disaster cannot be dismissed out of hand. Indeed, it's possible that the Crash of '08 is only the first of the dangerous perils that face the nation as the result of unsustainable economic inequality.

WHO WILL REBEL

Revolutions are most likely to occur when the middle class loses faith in the system of governance. Ironically, it

---

[*]   See Will & Ariel Durant, *The Lessons of History* (Simon & Schuster, 1968), 55–57.

[†]   WEF 2009, "Global crisis 'has destroyed 40pc of world wealth,' " *Telegraph* (U.K.), January 29, 2009 (reporting on discussion at the 2009 World Economic Forum in Davos, Switzerland).

is not the poor who will rebel: it is the middle class. Revolutions are born among dissatisfied, frustrated people.

Today, even President Obama has acknowledged that the middle class is suffering and experiencing "the American Dream in reverse."* The combination of extreme economic inequality and the impact of the financial crisis could push the former middle class to move from frustration to dangerous anger: an anger sparked by reduced circumstances, loss of faith in our economic system, and the belief that they have been treated unfairly as compared to the wealthier members of society.

As extreme inequality has evolved in the United States, the viability of a vibrant middle class—as it has traditionally been understood—has eroded. The American Dream is essentially a middle-class dream: a vision of economic security through steady employment, home ownership, modern medicine, retirement without worry, and the ability to send the kids to college. Sadly, the people that realize this vision are becoming a smaller and smaller segment of our population. More and more Americans are concluding that their children will live a less prosperous life than their own. If the middle class disappears, our society polarizes between the rich on one side and everyone else on the other side.

---

* As quoted in ABC News, "Obama: 'It's Like the American Dream in Reverse,'" January 30, 2009, http://blogs.abcnews.com/politicalpunch/2009/01/obama-its-like.html.

One widely accepted theory of the roots of revolutions holds that they occur when a specific group, such as the middle class, is led to believe conditions will improve, and then this promise is not realized. Call it the theory of crushed hopes. From this perspective the election of Barack Obama can be viewed as the moment of highest risk for the nation. The nation is suffering from the highest recorded level of economic inequality in our history, the middle class was suffering before the economic crisis and is now in dire straits, and President Obama campaigned on a promise to restore middle-class prosperity—thereby raising expectations. If the Obama administration does not succeed in raising the relative prosperity of the middle class, our nation will confront precisely the circumstances that often lead to revolutions: A downtrodden class is led to believe things will improve and then loses faith in the government when these expectations are not met.

Extreme inequality is a national security issue. It is a threat to the very survival of our nation, as we know it today. As this book will show, *we cannot survive* as a vibrant nation if economic inequality continues on its extreme course. Too often, we characterize economic inequality as principally a moral issue. In fact, economic inequality is not solely an issue of fairness. It is a transcendent danger that threatens our national security and the survival of our form of government.

This book is not a prediction. It is by no means a call for revolution. Quite the opposite: it is a warning. As an ardent capitalist, a patriot, a lawyer with a background in constitutional theory, and a student of our democracy who prizes our form of government, my intent in writing this book is to offer a wake-up call. The rewards of our current economy and the distribution of our national income are not sustainable. We are rapidly heading for political instability, which could ultimately lead to some form of revolution. The burden of this book is to demonstrate the significance and severity of the problem. At the end, I will offer some solutions to the problem of our increasing concentration of wealth, but there is no quick fix. The issues associated with economic inequality are complex and reflect a confluence of trends that have been building in our nation for the past 30 years.

The prodigious historians Will and Ariel Durant wrote a short book titled *The Lessons of History*, after studying the long sweep of history from Athens, through Rome, the Renaissance, and the founding of the United States. In the book, they quite correctly warn against the misuse of historical analogies, noting that "History is so indifferently rich that a case for almost any conclusion from it can be made by a selection of instances." Nonetheless, they cautiously proceed on "a precarious enterprise"* to identify common trends among multiple civilizations.

---

* Will and Ariel Durant, *The Lessons of History*, 13, 97.

The Durants' entire book is 102 pages, full of caveats about its few careful generalizations. The chapter "Economics and History," all of six pages, notes that civilizations of all types generally operate in cycles: first, a concentration of wealth. Next, its redistribution. The Durants touch on Plutarch, Solon the lawgiver in Athens, Roman history from Tiberius Grachuss (133 B.C.) through the Pax Romana (A.D. 180), the rise of the Catholic Church, the Reformation, the French Revolution, and the modern United States. Amidst this armada of civilizations the Durants' theme is that this cycle of economic history is a constant. The concluding paragraph of the chapter puts it this way:

> We conclude that the concentration of wealth is natural and inevitable and is periodically alleviated by violent or peaceable partial redistribution. In this view, all economic history is the slow heartbeat of the social organism, a vast systole and diastole of concentrating wealth and compulsive recirculation.

The Durants' analysis suggests that every few generations prosperous countries will face an inevitable need to ensure the equitable distribution of wealth. This process occurs with greater frequency in democracies. The Durants observe, "the rate of concentration [of wealth] varies (other factors being equal) with the economic freedom permitted by morals and laws. Despotism may for a time retard the concentration; democracy, allowing the most liberty, accelerates it."

The stark choice they present is that this balancing can happen peacefully or through violence.

In progressive societies the concentration may reach a point where the strength in numbers of the many poor rivals the strength in ability of the few rich; then the unstable equilibrium generates a critical situation, which history has diversely met by legislation redistributing wealth or by revolution distributing poverty.

The Durants recognize that the United States has faced this challenge in the past, and presciently predicted that the country would face it in the future. Writing in 1968, they said:

> The government of the United States, in 1933–52 and 1960–65, followed Solon's peaceful methods, and accomplished a moderate and pacifying redistribution; perhaps someone had studied history. The upper classes in America cursed, complied, and resumed the concentration of wealth.[*]

The lessons are clear: We may believe that the United States is immune to political instability and revolution, but if so, the United States is breaking all the rules of history.

---

[*]   Ibid., 55–57.

• • •

America is now battling the greatest financial crisis since the Great Depression. Millions of Americans have lost their homes, millions more are threatened with foreclosure. Millions of Americans have lost the ability to find a job that pays a decent wage. Millions of Americans have lost the retirement savings they prudently built while working for decades.

The relationship among economic inequality, revolutions, and economic shocks are explored at length in this book. There are two points worth noting at the start. First, an exhaustive look at the history of modern revolutions shows that, in most cases, they followed some form of serious, destabilizing, negative economic event. For example, the fall of the Soviet Union had far more to do with the collapse in the price of oil than with Ronald Reagan's military buildup. As a large exporter of oil, the Soviet Union's access to hard currency was crushed when the price of oil collapsed in the mid-1980s, which set off the chain of events that led to the dissolution of the nation. Two hundred years earlier, the French Revolution effectively began when Louis XVI convened the Assembly of Notables as a precursor to raising tax revenues. Ironically, France had gone bankrupt through heavy lending to the Colonists in our own bid for freedom.

An economic crisis puts stress on all aspects of a society, including its government: fear rises throughout the society, business relationships become strained or dissolve, anger rises, and anxiety increases everywhere. People typically turn to their government at moments of crisis—for much-needed assistance, for reform, and for a restoration of confidence in the future. What if the government fails them? In a war, citizens face physical risk but are likely to unite behind their government. In contrast, the multiple, frequently conflicting views and public emotions in an economic crisis can quickly lead to class warfare and other social crises. Often, the government is blamed, fairly or unfairly, for causing the crisis or for failing to prevent it. The result is that an economic crisis is frequently the catalyst that pushes a vulnerable political system over the edge from instability to revolution.

In America, there are indications that the Great Depression came closer to threatening our constitutional form of government than is generally acknowledged. Walter Lippman, one of the leading columnists of the era, wrote that "A mild form of dictatorship will help us over the roughest spots on the road ahead." In February 1932, before FDR's March inauguration, Lippman traveled to Georgia to meet with Roosevelt and tell him that he might have to assume the powers of a dictator for an uncertain length of time. One of FDR's biographers notes that "the columnist spoke for the American political establishment."* During the same period, violence broke

---

* Jonathan Alter, *The Defining Moment: FDR's Hundred Days and the Triumph of Hope* (Simon & Schuster, 2006), 187.

out throughout the farm belt,* and one of FDR's closest advisors told the president-elect two days after his election, "it must be remembered that by March 4 [inauguration day] next we may have anything on our hands from a recovery to a revolution. The chance is about even either way."† In 1932, Congressman Hamilton Fish, Jr., of New York said, "If we don't give it [dictatorship] under the existing system, the people will change the system." The following year, he wrote Roosevelt that Republicans were ready to "give you any power you need."‡ In his first inaugural address, FDR said that he might need to seek "broad executive power to wage war against the emergency." He is known to have considered, but rejected, using the word "dictatorship" in preparing the speech.§

Today, the economic crisis is a shock to a political system that is already weakened by extreme economic inequality. This combination of extreme economic inequality and a once-in-a-century economic crisis adds significantly to the overall risk now facing the survival of our form of government.

• • •

---

* See Jean Edward Smith, *FDR* (Random House, 2007), 290; and William Manchester, *The Glory and the Dream: A Narrative History of America 1932–1972* (Little, Brown, 1974), 58–60.

† Adolf Berle, quoted in David M. Kennedy, *Freedom from Fear: The American People in Depression and War, 1929–1945* (Oxford, 2005), 117.

‡ Manchester, *The Glory and the Dream,* 58.

§ Alter, *The Defining Moment,* 219.

One reason readers may find the ideas in this book shocking is that democracies are presumed to be self-correcting. Indeed, it can be argued that the larger the perceived problems, the stronger the likely response by the public at the ballot box. This is certainly the case today, as President Obama has a Democratic majority both in the house and in the Senate. The Democrats interpret the election of '08 as a historic shift: a decisive decision by the public to move away from the anything-goes deregulation era initiated by the 1980 election of Ronald Reagan. Should we not assume that the stultifying effects of polarization in Washington have now ended, and that the necessary remedial action for our many problems will soon be forthcoming?

The idea that American politics move according to this self-correcting ebb and flow is the central notion of Arthur Schlesinger's book *The Cycles of American History*. Schlesinger concludes that the threat of revolution is actually a part of the democratic process, serving as the ultimate reason for dissenting parties to agree upon reforms. Schlesinger writes:

[T]he revolutionary challenge undermines the obstacles of imbecility and vested interest. The threat of violence may smooth the way for persuasion. Even the most intractable conservative, his back against the wall, will accept reform as an alternative to revolution. "Since the times of Rameses," commented Henry Adams, "revolutions have raised more doubts than they solved, but they sometimes have the merits of changing one's point of view."*

While I fervently hope that Schlesinger's observations remain appropriate for another 200-plus years, there are reasons to question their application to today's climate.

Extreme economic inequality has been building in the United States for over 30 years. The issues associated with this phenomenon are intimately tied to many of the most difficult problems facing our nation, including access to adequate healthcare and the skyrocketing federal debt, just to name two. Fundamentally, democracies are not good at long-term initiatives. The American political process is short-term-oriented. In order to get elected, and stay elected, our politicians must first focus on the immediate, short-term demands of their constituents.

In essence, even within the context of a democracy that has given an elected government a mandate for change, our inability to develop, implement, and sustain long-term initiatives may prevent the successful operation of the seemingly natural forces within democracies that self-correct for earlier mistakes.

At the same time, the Obama government has other priorities it must address—which will consume its energy, financial resources, and political capital. Second, even if Obama does develop and successfully implement a plan

---

* Arthur M. Schlesinger, Jr., *The Cycles of American History* (Houghton Mifflin, 1986), 427.

to rebuild economic equality in the nation it is likely to require a long-term commitment that extends beyond his tenure. Future presidents and legislators will need to maintain this priority in the face of competing demands and limited resources.

There are, in addition, at least two other reasons that our democracy may not self-correct for economic inequality. First, there is always the potential that our best efforts will not solve the problems—we will choose the wrong policies, implement the wrong reforms. Economic inequality is a complex problem, which is combined with the seemingly intractable issues of creating good jobs for displaced workers and ensuring the continuing prosperity of the disappearing middle class. It is by no means clear that our lawmakers have the appropriate solutions to these difficult challenges.

Second, there is the possibility that despite a public mandate for change, wealthy constituencies will employ their influence as large campaign donors, and through their lobbyists, prevent the adoption of meaningful government policies. As Senator Jim Webb writes in *A Time to Fight: Reclaiming a Fair and Just America,*

> No aristocracy in history has decided to give up any portion of its power willingly . . . Let's take it a step further . . . We should not hold our collective breaths upon the possibility that altruism will become a dominant theme in the campaign finance process. Politics is a transactional enter-

prise. And those who have power, wealth, and influence are rarely interested in losing those advantages.*

Americans are raised to believe that America holds a special place in the world. At times of worldwide turmoil, America is generally seen as the most stable of nations. As a consequence, the very idea of political instability may seem incredible. Yet the global financial meltdown demonstrates that there are societal contagions that can lead once-strong institutions to collapse. We know that extreme economic inequality is a long-term, complex, and immensely difficult problem for our society. There will always be priorities that seem more pressing, or appear to be a better use of resources. Nonetheless, a long-term view of our history and the history of other nations suggests that the longer we sweep this problem under the rug the greater the ultimate peril for the nation.

---

*   Jim Webb, *A Time to Fight: Reclaiming a Fair and Just America* (Broadway, 2008), 108.

LESSONS FROM THE SOVIET COLLAPSE

Consider just one recent example of a once-strong political state. Almost 20 years have passed since the Soviet Union lowered its flag for the final time. A study of what we know (or perhaps what we believe we know) about the fall of this superpower is highly revealing. The Soviet Union was the largest, most powerful nation to collapse unaided by war with a foreign power in the modern era. Hardly anyone thought it could happen there. Yet it did. The story of 1991 has six lessons that might apply to the United States today.[*]

First, the collapse of a nation-state does not necessarily involve violence.

The Soviet drama included one dramatic confrontation and some sporadic violence in outlying regions of the country. However, the confrontation ended without bloodshed and the violence that did take place—while it should not be trivialized—was a series of limited events.

In essence, once the Soviet Union as a governing body lost legitimacy in the eyes of its citizens, the leaders could

---

[*]   I would like to thank Rebekah M. Judson, who served as my research assistant for the section of the book addressing the collapse of the Soviet Union. Her research skills and understanding of Soviet history substantially enhanced this material.

only maintain power through brute force—involving horrible bloodshed, massive arrests, and deportations—assuming the army would even have *executed* such orders.

The central test of the peaceful versus violent dissolution of the country occurred with the failed coup in August 1991. Conservatives wanted to reestablish the old authoritarian regime and seized power. During this three-day confrontation, General Secretary Mikhail Gorbachev was under house arrest in the countryside in Foros, while Boris Yeltsin emerged as the pro-democratic leader in Moscow. Yeltsin set up headquarters in the White House, a Moscow building where the Russian parliament met.

As Robert Strayer writes in *Why Did the Soviet Union Collapse?*, Yeltsin "proclaimed all decrees of the Emergency Committee illegal, demanded the return of the country's legal president, and asked for massive civil disobedience." One result was that "ordinary people, perhaps fifty thousand to seventy thousand at any one time . . . came to defend the White House . . . They built barricades, tracked the movement of troops . . . and waited for what they expected would be a deadly assault." However:

> Unlike the Chinese leadership in Tienanmen Square protests in 1989, those centrally involved in the Soviet coup were either unable or unwilling to move beyond intimidation to violent repression and large-scale bloodshed. The horrible excesses of Stalinism . . . had rendered violence and bloodshed so illegitimate that even the coup leaders shrank from using it.

As resistance to the coup progressed, various security forces also changed sides to avoid "the price in bloodshed the coup leaders would have had to pay to enforce their rule." Tank teams in Moscow changed allegiances to protect the White House, the Soviet air force moved to protect the White House, and officers started to refuse to carry out orders. In the end, no lasting attack on the White House occurred. The coup ended with its leaders being arrested or committing suicide. The final dissolution of the Union of Soviet Socialist Republics (U.S.S.R.), by which fifteen republics each became independent states, officially occurred on December 25, 1991, when the Soviet Union's red banner was brought down the flagpole atop the Kremlin for the last time.[*]

Second, it is striking that neither the United States nor its Western allies appear to have anticipated, in any meaningful way, the fall of the Soviet Union.

In the late 1980s, the United States spent approximately $30 billion per year on intelligence, whose principal purpose was to analyze what was happening in the U.S.S.R.[†] Despite this extraordinary commitment of resources, the United States did not receive any advance warning of the impending collapse of the Soviet Union. Top officials in the

---

[*] Robert Strayer, *Why Did the Soviet Union Collapse?* (M.E. Sharpe, 1998), 3, 190–193.

[†] David Arbel and Ran Edelist, *Western Intelligence and the Collapse of the Soviet Union, 1980–1990: Ten Years That Did Not Shake the World* (Routledge, 2003), xi.

United States, interviewed after the fact, freely admitted that they were surprised by this turn of events.

Subsequent studies of why U.S. Sovietologists entirely missed the coming collapse of the U.S.S.R. concluded that, by and large, U.S. experts were *asking themselves the wrong questions* as the implosion approached. In the post-1988 period, Soviet experts were still debating whether the Soviet Union could undergo real reforms as opposed to broader questions associated with the long-term stability of the nation.* The continuing existence of the Soviet Union was essentially taken as a foregone conclusion.

When it comes to large, established nations there is a natural bias in favor of the status quo. Observers assume that these nations will continue to exist essentially in the same form. As a result, they reject information that might lead to a different, radical conclusion.

Third, revolutions often occur as a result of unplanned reactions to a series of cascading events, rather than a grand plot by those who end up in power.

We often confuse the idea of a revolution with a pre-planned coup. We tend to think of revolutions as necessarily involving plots with detailed timing and organization. Mao and Fidel Castro are thought to have

---

* Christopher I. Xenakis, *What Happened to the Soviet Union? How and Why American Sovietologists Were Caught by Surprise* (Praeger, 2002), 210.

single-handedly rallied communists to overthrow the governments of China and Cuba. In fact many revolutions occur as one event leads to another which leads to another, forcing a weakened political system over the edge of control.

In the Soviet Union, Gorbachev initiated a series of reforms aimed at establishing openness and revitalizing the economy. He soon faced a growing restlessness among the 15 republics. A dramatic economic shock—in the form of falling oil prices—reduced Russia's access to hard currency. All of these events played a role in the eventual collapse of the Soviet Union. It can be argued that Gorbachev's reforms may be the central factor that started this process, but there was certainly no central revolutionary, such as Lenin or Kerensky, who initiated and pushed this series of events. The idea that events build upon themselves does not mean that individuals don't opportunistically take advantage of situations as they present themselves. Certainly, Yeltsin's three-day stand at the White House in Russia dramatically enhanced his standing in the nation. But he did not initiate the chain of events that led to this historic confrontation. Similarly, the leaders of the individual Soviet republics pressed their desire for sovereignty, with increasingly public demonstrations, once momentum was moving in this direction. But they were opportunistically responding to events rather than guiding them.

Fourth, expensive and often unpopular foreign adventurism weakens domestic regimes.

Since the fall of Rome, historians have recognized that funding expensive foreign military activities can weaken domestic regimes. Rome's collapse is generally attributed, in part, to the cost of maintaining its empire, and associated foreign wars, at a time when the military was not enjoying the success of earlier generations. The Soviet Union's foray into Afghanistan is a clear example of this phenomenon. Over time, the war became less and less popular as it sapped the nation of able-bodied men, as the public increasingly came to view the war as unwinnable, and as it became ever more clear that vast resources were being emptied into what seemed like a bottomless pit. Since the Soviet economy was performing poorly, citizens became particularly resentful of the large expenditures pouring into Afghanistan at the expense of domestic improvements. Ultimately, after a ten-year involvement that resulted in 36,000 dead or wounded Soviet men and women, and about one million dead or wounded Afghanis, the Soviet Union pulled out of the region.* The Middle East has traditionally been "the graveyard of empire." From Alexander the Great to Julius Ceasar to Napoleon, from the British Empire to the Soviet Union, all came to the Middle East and

---

* Richard Rhodes, *Arsenals of Folly* (Knopf, 2007), 284.

"failed, frequently bringing down their own empires in the process.'"*

Fifth, an economic shock that leads to the loss of domestic economic security is a powerful destabilizing force on any political regime.

The Soviet Union's economic rigidity played an obvious role in its collapse. The political structure of the nation was dramatically weakened by its dysfunctional economy. Moreover, history is replete with examples of revolutions that were triggered by economic shocks. In essence, ongoing national security—which is often seen solely in terms of foreign policy—also requires domestic economic strength and stability. Yegor Gaidar, who served as acting prime minister of Russia, minister of economy, and first deputy prime minister between 1991 and 1994, attributes the collapse of the Soviet Union to the sudden decline in oil prices in the 1980s. The nation's dysfunctional economy relied on oil revenues for purchases of foreign grain. Gaidar asserts, "The timeline of the collapse of the Soviet Union can be traced to Sept. 13, 1985," when Saudi Arabia announced it would "stop protecting oil prices." As a result, "the Soviet Union lost approximately $20 billion per year, money without which

---

* Rufus Fears, *The Wisdom of History, Part 1 of 3* (course transcript) (The Teaching Company, 2007), 9.

the country simply could not survive." By 1989, the Soviet Union needed to borrow $100 million annually from the West to finance grain purchases. According to Gaidar, at this time it became understood that a condition of these funds would be that the Soviet regime would not use force to prop up communist regimes in Eastern Europe or ultimately repress independence movements within the Soviet empire.[*]

Sixth, revolutions often occur in the midst of a reform movement.

Revolutions often start with reform efforts by the existing leadership. At some point, the national leadership loses control. Gorbachev was a reformer who wanted to save communism, not destroy it. But he could only raise the people's hopes by liberating the press (to a degree), and he could not quickly restructure the economy. Russian historian Edvard Radzisky paraphrases a classic Russian saying (which he applied to reformist Tsar Alexander II): "Starting reforms in Russia is dangerous. But it is much more dangerous to stop them."

---

[*]   Yegor Gaidar, "The Soviet Collapse: Grain and Oil," working paper, American Enterprise Institute Issues, April 2007. See also Yegor Gaidar, *Collapse of an Empire: Lessons for Modern Russia* (Brookings, 2007).

• • •

The United States is not the Soviet Union. Our economy is not as terrible. Our government is not as despised. But nobody thought the U.S.S.R. could collapse. Could everyone be wrong again?

CHAPTER THREE

THE CAUSES OF REVOLUTIONS

INTRODUCTION

Revolutions are rare events. Like earthquakes, they can occur with limited warning, and forever shift the landscape beneath them.

Since the days of Aristotle and probably earlier, people have pondered the causes of political instability and governmental collapse. In the modern era, reams of academic papers and books authored by historians, sociologists, political scientists, and economists have put forth a wide range of theories asserting why revolutions occur. Human behavior is inherently difficult to predict, and many of these theories of revolution are conflicting or limited in their actual usefulness. There is no consensus among social scientists on why revolutions occur.

Nonetheless, a close reading of history and the theories of the best social scientists can provide, if not a precise formula, at least some common conditions that dramatically increase the risk of political instability. Let's call them risk factors, rather than absolute causes. The more risk factors present at any one moment, and the greater their severity, the more likely political instability and revolution will ultimately occur. It's like assessing the risk of a heart attack: an individual with no family history of coronary disease, who exercises regularly, eats healthfully, and maintains an appropriate weight, is highly unlikely to suffer, whereas someone who has a family history of heart disease, is grossly overweight, never exercises, consumes too much alcohol, and suffers from high blood pressure is, if not guaranteed, highly likely to suffer.

The aim of this chapter is to identify the circumstances that are most likely to indicate the potential for revolution in the United States. The goal is to develop a checklist of risk factors. The more of them present in any society, the exponentially greater the risk. From Aristotle to modern historians, five particular risk factors have received special attention: (1) the distribution of wealth and the health of the middle class, (2) the impact of recent economic or political shocks, (3) the lack of satisfaction of rising expectations, (4) the perception of unfairness in the distribution of wealth, and (5) the history and efficacy of institutions in the society.

Before turning to these factors, we need, however, to define what is and isn't a revolution. Here is a short list of grand historical revolutions: the English Revolution in 1640, the American Revolution in 1776, the French Revolution in 1789, the Russian Revolution in 1917, and China's Communist Revolution in 1949.* But what about Hitler's takeover of the former Weimar Republic, or the fall of the Soviet Union in 1991? They also led to dramatic changes in the way societies governed themselves. Should we consider them all to be political revolutions?

For my purposes, extreme violence is not necessary. I take revolution to mean "the overthrow of one government or governmental system and its replacement with another." This is a highly inclusive definition. It does not require that revolutions be initiated by a mass movement. Hitler's takeover counts. Although the titles, e.g., chancellor, may not have changed, the system of government certainly did.

THE DISTRIBUTION OF WEALTH AND THE IMPORTANCE OF THE MIDDLE CLASS

Over the 2,500 years since Aristotle, the historiography of revolutions has evolved markedly. However, the one conclusion that has never changed is that economic inequality plays a central role in political instability.

---

* See Martin Malia and Terence Emmons, eds., *History's Locomotives: Revolutions and the Making of the Modern World* (Yale, 2006), 287.

This link was recognized by the ancient Greeks and Romans. The classical historian Plutarch observed that "An imbalance between rich and poor is the oldest and most fatal ailments of all republics." As one scholar has noted, for Aristotle, "economic disparities did not simply spell injustice, they were the prelude to a breakdown of the cohesion that held society together."[*] In the current era, social scientists continuously reaffirm this conclusion.

Political scientists and economists have worked to verify this conclusion statistically. For example, two leading economists created a cross-national database to quantify the degree of political instability in 60 or more countries at different time periods. Harvard economics professor Alberto Alessina and Italian economist Roberto Perotti explain the findings of this work as follows, "Income inequality increases social discontent and fuels social unrest. The latter, by increasing the probability of coups, revolutions, [and] mass violence."[†] When economic inequality within a democracy reaches a certain level, the basic functioning

---

[*]   Michael Thompson, *The Politics of Inequality: A Political History of the Idea of Economic Inequality in America* (Columbia University, 2007), 34.

[†]   Alberto Alessina and Roberto Perotti, "Income Distribution, Political Instability and Investment," *European Economic Review* 40 (June 1996): 1202–29. See also, Edward Muller and Mitchell Seligson, "Inequality and Insurgency," *American Political Science Review* 81, no. 2 (June 1987); Bruce Russert, "Inequality and Instability: The Relation of Land Tenure to Politics," *World Politics* 16, no. 3 (April 1964): 442–454; and Fred Cort, "The Quantification of Aristotle's Theory of Revolution," *American Political Science Review* 46, no. 2 (June 1952): 491 (discussing the earlier work of Harold Davis in *Political Statistics*, 1948).

of the society breaks down. Robert Reich, the former U.S. secretary of labor, states the problem simply but powerfully: "After a point, as inequality widened, the bonds that kept our society together would snap. Every decision we tried to arrive at together . . . would be harder to make because it would have such different consequences for the relatively rich than for the relatively poor . . . We would begin to lose our capacity for democratic governance."[*]

Here's how this governance problem can evolve: As inequality rises, two phenomena almost always occur: The wealthy develop a sense of entitlement, and they increasingly seek to insulate themselves from the rest of society. They live in exclusive communities; socialize with each other; send their children to private schools, exclusive, locally funded public schools, and elite colleges; and can afford top-quality healthcare and medical insurance. As a consequence, they become less dependent on public services and less connected to the concerns of the rest of society. Inevitably, this leads the bulk of those in the top income strata to oppose tax increases that would fund enhanced public amenities. Instead, they use their wealth to obtain political influence that solidifies their privileges. At this point, the divided nation becomes polarized and the government becomes incapable of decisive action. This is a simplistic model—yet a fundamentally accurate

---

[*]   Robert Reich, *I'll Be Short: Essentials for a Decent Working Society* (Beacon, 2002), 19–20.

description of what has happened in America over the past 30 years.

The flip side of the danger of extreme economic inequality is the recognition that a strong middle class is essential. Perhaps surprisingly, this recognition goes back at least to the ancient Greeks and Aristotle. In Aristotle's view, no lasting democracy could exist as a polarized society of rich and poor: a vibrant and large middle class was essential. In writing about "The Most Practicable Type of Constitution," Aristotle concluded:

> It is clear from our argument . . . that good government is attainable in those states where there is a large middle class—large enough, if possible, to be stronger than both of the other classes, but at any rate large enough to be stronger than either of them singly; for in that case its addition to either will suffice to turn the scale, and will prevent either of the opposing extremes from becoming dominant. It is therefore the greatest of blessings for a state that its members should possess a moderate and adequate property . . .
>
> The reason why democracies are generally more secure and more permanent than oligarchies is the character of their middle class, which is more numerous, and is allowed a larger share in the government, than it is in oligarchies. *Where democracies have no middle class, and the poor are greatly superior*

in number, trouble ensues and they are speedily ruined.
[emphasis added]*

Aristotle's analysis has withstood the test of time. At the end of a nearly 400-page history of the role of the middle class in democracy, one scholar concludes, "Thus, history has shown us that an economic and political framework conducive to democracy may be established, but if the class base of that society is skewed toward the rich or the poor, the democracy will not remain stable. This, of course, is right out of the Aristotelian theory with which we began this volume."†

In 1831 and early 1832, Alexis de Toqueville toured America and subsequently wrote *Democracy in America*, which has been called the best book ever written about both America and democracy. In a chapter titled "Why Great Revolutions Will Become Rare," de Tocqueville similarly concluded that the middle class is the great bulwark that protects democracy in a society: "It is the poor who have wanted to rob the rich or the rich who have tried to put the poor in chains. Therefore, if you can found a state of society in which each has something to keep and little to take [i.e., a middle class], you will have done much for the peace of the world."‡

* Aristotle, *The Politics*, as excerpted in Michael Curtis, ed., *The Great Political Theories* (Avon, 1961), 94–95.
† Ronald M. Glassman, *The Middle Class and Democracy in Socio-Historical Perspective* (E.J. Brill, 1995), 379.
‡ Alexis de Tocqueville, *Democracy in America* (University of Chicago Press, 2000), 607.

Today, the very real threat to America is that we will reach a tipping point where middle-class prosperity is so weakened and membership so depleted that Aristotle's warning becomes a prediction. Lou Dobbs, the CNN anchor, has argued forcefully for several years that the middle class is collapsing downward. Now, as the economic crisis accelerates financial pressure on middle-class families, many more analysts are starting to sound just like him.* The American Dream is, at its core, a middle-class dream. Although it is stated in several variants, it consists of five basic components: job security (or, at least, solid job prospects), owning a home, a pension or adequate retirement, the ability to send the kids to college, and upward mobility (the expectation that life will materially improve for each generation). This dream is what sustains American capitalism. If the middle class disappears, the American Dream will disappear along with it. It is impossible to imagine that our nation could sustain our democracy in anything like its current form if that should happen. America cannot exist principally as a nation of haves and have nots without the broad middle. In such a world, all types of previously unimaginable scenarios become possible.

---

* See Lou Dobbs, *War on the Middle Class: How the Government, Big Business, and Special Interest Groups Are Waging War on the American Dream and How to Fight Back* (Penguin, 2006).

ECONOMIC OR POLITICAL SHOCKS

Perhaps the most well-documented precursor to revolution is a sudden political or economic shock. Sudden shocks that create mass suffering, anger, and lack of trust serve to destabilize society's institutions. Every weak point in a nation's governmental system is tested by severe trauma.

The most fundamental responsibility of a national government is to provide for the physical safety of its citizens. In the fictional scenario at the start of this book, the federal government failed in this task. As a consequence, the national government was replaced by independent state governments simply because they could stave off attack.

Yet revolutions do not necessarily require a political shock as dramatic as a bombing. The potential for a severe *economic* shock to undermine the stability of a long-standing national government has been demonstrated throughout history: the French Revolution of 1789 began when the national government effectively declared that it was bankrupt; the Soviet Union fell in large part because oil revenues, which supported the bulk of the economy, declined dramatically, leading, in part, to severe inflation; the hyperinflation that accompanied the Weimar Republic opened the door to the Nazi victory and dissolution of the newly established German democracy. The extent to which an economic shock can lead to political instability depends on three things: the extent of the suffering of the people, the trust of the people in the existing government, and the degree to which the tragedy had been anticipated or expected. It is not absolute suffering that matters so much as relative deprivation. You don't have to starve, you just have to be a lot worse off than you expected. The more unexpected the shock, the more anger-provoking the results.

After World War I, hyperinflation in Germany led to extreme suffering. At the same time, the replacement of the Kaiser by the Allied-inspired Weimar Republic created a government that was distrusted and unable to alleviate the situation. While suffering in the face of defeat may not have been unexpected, the extreme level of the suffering, and the lack of trust in the system of government, created an environment that was well-suited to the emergence of a savior who could restore prosperity. Hitler was easily able to ignore the nascent provisions of the Weimar Constitution. After obtaining office through legal means, he had no trouble establishing a constitutionally illegal dictatorship.

In the French Revolution, all three factors established an atmosphere that facilitated the downfall of the monarchy. By the time of the revolution, the debt of the French monarchy had reached the point where over half of annual revenues went to debt service, a large portion of the coming year's income had already been spent, and the monarchy was finding it increasingly difficult to borrow, even at "ruinous rates of interest." This effective bankruptcy and credit strike forced Louis XVI to convene the Estates General. Poor harvests made things worse. In 1788, when the harvest failed, the price of bread skyrocketed, and "demand for manufactured commodities collapsed, so the laboring poor were denied employment just when they needed it most." Violence erupted throughout the country. There was also an overwhelming lack of trust in government among the lower classes. Rumors circulated that the government was attempting to starve the population into submission. The riots reflected both fear of famine and hatred of those seen as exploiters. Finally, trust was further eroded by an antiquated tax system and a lack of disclosure regarding the true state of the king's finances. The mass of taxpayers believed that the aristocracy was propped up on the backs of commoners. Extreme suffering, massive distrust, and anger led directly to revolution.*

The Soviet regime never established much trust in government. As the tightly integrated Soviet economy unraveled, annual inflation exceeded 50 percent in 1990, and reached between 600 and 700 percent in 1991. Unemployment increased, a crisis for a society that promised everyone a job. Significant segments of the population were suddenly paying between 60 and 80 percent of their income for food. As Strayer has noted, "the Soviet economic crisis had produced an embittered and angry population, most of whom saw themselves as victims of perestroika rather

---

* Tim Blanning, *The Pursuit of Glory: The Five Revolutions That Made Modern Europe 1648–1815* (Penguin, 2007), 337–338.

than beneficiaries."* In a few short years, the nation went from the expectation of a new, brighter future to a deep and unexpected misery. In this context, the ultimate fall of the government seems all but inevitable.

More recently, the administration of President Obama has recognized the potentially central role of severe economic shock as a cause of political instability or revolution. Each year, the director of national intelligence is required to provide Congress with an "Annual Threat Assessment." In his first appearance before the Senate Select Committee on Intelligence in February 2009 to deliver this assessment, Dennis Blair told the legislators that instability around the world, caused by the current global economic crisis, as opposed to terrorism, is now the primary near-term threat to the security of the United States. Citing "the dramatic political consequences wrought by the economic turmoil of the 1920s and 1930s in Europe, the instability, and high levels of violent extremism," Blair went on to say that "Roughly a quarter of the countries in the world have already experienced low-level instability such as government changes because of the current slowdown. Europe and the former Soviet Union have experienced the bulk of the anti-state demonstrations." He warned that "Statistical modeling shows that economic crises increase the risk of regime-threatening instability if they persist over a one-to-two-year period."†

---

* Strayer, *Why Did the Soviet Union Collapse?*, 136–137.
† See "Financial Crisis Called Top Security Threat to U.S.," *Washington Post,*

The problem with social science, of course, is that you cannot run historical experiments. History provides one set of facts, and we can only wonder about alternatives. But let's consider one "counterfactual": the Great Depression in America. Why *didn't* this economic shock lead to a revolution?

First, the central point of this analysis is *not* that risk factors in this discussion will automatically result in a revolution; rather, they increase the odds. A nation can be in a high-risk situation and still escape catastrophe. Obviously Roosevelt, supported by Congress, was able to take the actions necessary to prevent a revolution.

Roosevelt did recognize the possibility of a revolution when he entered office. After his election, but before his inauguration, violence broke out in the farm belt, and magazines such as *Harper's, Atlantic, Scribner's,* and others all debated "the imminence" of revolution. According to one widely repeated newspaper report, a visitor told FDR, "Mr. President, if your program succeeds, you'll be the greatest president in American history." "If it fails," FDR replied, "I'll be the *last* one."[*]

But Roosevelt worked hard to increase economic equality, and during his tenure, inequality decreased dramatically.[†] Roosevelt supported programs ranging from the creation of

---

February 13, 2009; and Dennis Blair, Director of National Intelligence, *Annual Threat Assessment of the Intelligence Community for the Senate Select Committee on Intelligence,* February 12, 2009.

[*]   Alter, *The Defining Moment,* 6, 186.

[†]   When Roosevelt entered office in 1933, the top 10 percent of American families accounted for 46 percent of all income; this had decreased to 33 percent by 1944. Saez, "Striking It Richer."

the modern-day social safety net at the bottom of the income ladder, to steady increases in the highest marginal tax rates at the top. Before his death, he envisioned an economic bill of rights that would have had an even broader impact on equal opportunity than the GI Bill, which effectively provided a college education to an entire generation that would have otherwise found college out of reach. Many regard the GI Bill as the single greatest piece of social legislation in the twentieth century. It was actually a watered-down version of the grander "economic bill of rights" that Roosevelt envisioned in his 1944 State of the Union message to Congress, which Roosevelt read over the radio in order to reach the public.*

Finally, FDR positioned himself as a radical defender of the interests of the people. Roosevelt's campaign for a second term included such strong rhetoric as an attack on the "economic royalists" who possessed the concentrated wealth of the nation, and the statement that "powerful influences" that seek to restore a government that is "indifferent" are "unanimous in their hatred for me—and I welcome their hatred."† Of great importance, FDR's legislative initiatives matched his rhetoric. His speeches were more than empty talk. He initiated a legislative agenda that matched his public stance. By moving so far left, FDR effectively prevented alternative political initiatives from gaining adherents.

---

* See Edward Humes, *Over Here: How the G.I. Bill Transformed the American Dream* (Harcourt, 2006), 197. Frank Freidel, *Franklin D. Roosevelt* (Little, Brown, 1990), 499–500.

† Jean Edward Smith, *FDR*, 372–373.

In summary, a severe political or economic shock has, throughout history, been a central cause of revolutions. We are already witnessing labor unrest in Greece, eastern Europe, France, even China. Could it happen here?

THE FAILURE OF RISING EXPECTATIONS

Revolutions often result when societies experience a period of rising expectations followed by a sudden, unexpected failure to meet them. When people anticipate a better life and their hopes are suddenly dashed, the stage is set for radical change.*

As de Tocqueville observed, with puzzlement, the French Revolution occurred after a period of sustained improvement in lifestyles. In effect, this period set the stage. Once the hope of a better life was dashed, anger and frustration boiled over as it never would have had expectations been lower. This model fits the Soviet Union as well. While Gorbachev initially raised people's hopes, the subsequent collapse of the economy made the freedoms enjoyed under glasnost all the more frustrating. Expectations of a better life were summarily destroyed.

---

* See James C. Davies, "Toward a Theory of Revolutions," *American Sociological Review* 6, no. 1 (February 1962): 5–19. For an overview of the scholarly debate surrounding many of the ideas discussed in this chapter, see Stephen K. Sanderson, *Revolutions: A Worldwide Introduction to Political and Social Change* (Paradigm, 2005), 61–73.

Revolutions occur—or do not occur—because people *believe* in something. Mobility in the United States is actually lower than mobility in almost all European countries and Canada, despite the abiding myth of the Horatio Alger rags-to-riches story.* The myth is more important than the reality. As long as we *believe* that the United States is the land of opportunity, then we will remain loyal. But if that belief collapses, watch out.

The theory of rising expectations also explains a second seemingly puzzling aspect of revolutions: As in the Soviet example, they often occur during or immediately following periods of reform. Times of reform are actually destabilizing. When the leadership of a society acknowledges that changes are needed, and people come to expect something new and better, the reforms had better deliver. If this process is derailed for any reason, overwhelming anger and frustration can lead to revolution. *A period of significant reform is therefore a moment of potentially maximum risk.*

RELATIVE DEPRIVATION: THE PERCEPTION OF UNFAIRNESS

In 1970, Ted Robert Gurr published *Why Men Rebel*, which

---

*   See, for example, Jo Blanden, Paul Gregg, and Stephen Machin, *Intergenerational Mobility in Europe and North America*, Centre for Economic Performance, London School of Economics, April 2005.

argued that it is not the absolute level of misery that matters. Instead, it is the level of dissatisfaction individuals—or a group—feel *relative to what they expected from life* that counts.* Gurr grounded his ideas in what sociologists called *relative deprivation*.

The general concept of relative deprivation holds that it is not the *absolute* well-being of a group or individuals, but their *relative* well-being that determines the likelihood that they will experience dissatisfaction. This is similar to the previous point about expectations. The absolute facts matter less than perceptions and (in this case) *context*. Revolutions can happen in societies that are affluent compared to the rest of the world: people get frustrated within a frame of reference, not within a global database. It is a fundamental aspect of human nature to look at how we are doing and compare our own well-being with those around us.

The question is, what is your frame of reference? My belief on this point is at odds with the mainstream view. Many scholars hold that in difficult times, middle-class families don't really compare their well-being to upper-class families; they compare their well-being to other members of the middle class. These scholars assert that individuals are more apt to compare their situation to their neighbors than to an unknown member of a far wealthier class, such as a hedge-fund owner. Yet, over the past 20 years, America has developed a consumer culture

---

* Ted Robert Gurr, *Why Men Rebel* (Princeton, 1970).

that encourages everyone to believe they *should* be living, at minimum, the American Dream: Commercials are effectively aimed at the buying power of those at the eightieth percentile of income.

The media fixation with celebrity and wealth has also given Americans an ongoing look at the lives of those at the top. In good times and bad, we are bombarded with stories of how the "rich and famous" are living. The media has a seemingly insatiable desire to report that "while you are suffering, the rich and famous are relaxing on the beach in . . . ".* At a time of stress and possibly growing political instability, such journalism has the potential to dangerously inflame public opinion.

POLITICAL INSTITUTIONS: HISTORY AND COMPETENCE

The influence of political institutions on their own survival is complex but, by and large, breaks down into four central questions:

---

* See, for example, this report at the *Daily Beast*, a Web magazine, on the wife of Dick Fuld, the disgraced CEO of Lehman Brothers, purchasing three $2,250 cashmere Hermès scarves at one of her regular visits to the store, but choosing a plain shopping bag to hide her spending. The article states, "Since the Lehman Brothers bankruptcy, Mrs. Fuld has still been a regular client, visiting the boutique once a week and spending $5,000 or $10,000 each time, says the associate. Now, she doesn't want anyone to know." http://www.thedailybeast.com/ blogs-and-stories/2008–12–15/shopping-in-secret/.

First, what is the political history of the society? The newer the political system the greater its inherent risk. Systems that have survived for hundreds of years are far more likely to command allegiance and have a proven ability to adapt to change. This is particularly true for a democracy. The sheer fact that the Constitution has prospered for over two centuries makes discussion of political instability in the United States seem far-fetched. Americans accord high respect to their history and form of government. Moreover, part of the genius of the Constitution was the incorporation of the amendment process. The founders provided for an orderly process to adapt the rules of government to changing circumstances. With a built-in mechanism for revising our system of governance, who needs revolution?

Second, to what extent is a government willing to use violence and repression against its own population to stay in power? It is unlikely that free expression in America would be curtailed or that armed forces (broadly defined as the U.S. military, the National Guard, or the police) would fire on Americans unless some form of rampant violence or destruction of property took place. In the event popular opinion were to shift away from our form of government, a nonviolent collapse similar to the Soviet Union's is much more likely than a violent one.

Third, how well is the government functioning? This question has particular relevance for America today. The Roman Republic was transformed from a thriving republic to a dictatorship largely because of extreme polarization.

While scholars cite many reasons for the demise of the Republic, the underlying problem was the Senate's inability to address a range of difficult problems, such as the need to make provisions for returning army veterans.* Ultimately, it was this paralysis in the government's ability to function that caused Rome's republican form of government to fail.

The 110th Congress, which operated in 2007 and 2008, had the fewest legislative accomplishments of any Congress since World War II.† Prior to the Democratic sweep in late 2008, our national government had ceased to effectively function, in part because of extreme polarization between Democrats and Republicans.

The ability of a government to function is also based on its basic competence. The failure of the Bush administration was widely seen as a case of gross incompetence: The nation expected a swifter and better response to the tragedy of Katrina; and the nation was divided on the Iraq War and turned against it when the occupation seemed incompetent. The improvement in Iraqi security and politics in 2007–2008 did little to regain popular support, which had been squandered. If the U.S. government fails to keep Americans safe from terrorism at home, its fundamental competence would be widely questioned.

Fourth, are political institutions able to adapt suffi-

---

* Jurgen von Urgen-Sternberg, *The Crisis of the Republic,* in Harriet I. Flower, ed., *The Cambridge Companion to the Roman Republic* (Cambridge, 2004), 106.

† "As U.S. Economic Problems Loom, House, Senate Sweat the Small Stuff," *Wall Street Journal,* August 19, 2008.

ciently swiftly to changing realities? In 1997, two years before his death, the eminent historian Arthur Schlesinger, Jr., published an essay in *Foreign Affairs* titled "Has Democracy a Future?" This essay reviewed the progress of democracy throughout the twentieth century, and concluded its future was by no means guaranteed.

One challenge is what Schlesinger calls "The Law of Acceleration." He noted that "Modern democracy itself is the political offspring of technology and capitalism, the two most dynamic—that is to say, destabilizing—forces loose in the world today. Both are driven ever onward by self-generated momentum that strains the bonds of social control and of political sovereignty."* Today, it is reasonable to say that the majority of economists believe that the current economic crisis reflects, at least in large measure, a failure on the part of the government to adapt to changes in the financial system. This led to an unregulated world of "shadow banking" with disastrous consequences.

THE IMPORTANCE OF TRUST

As a general rule, scholars who have studied the dynamics of political instability and revolutions have downplayed the role of trust in institutions, such as government and

---

* Arthur M. Schlesinger, Jr., "Has Democracy a Future?" *Foreign Affairs*, September/October 1997.

business, as a central causal factor. Rather, the collapse of trust is generally linked to the rising anger that accompanies the causal mechanisms described above, such as failed expectations during a period of reform, relative deprivation, or a lack of institutional competence. But is lack of trust an artifact? Or a cause in and of itself?

There is no question that the loss of trust inevitably accompanies revolutionary situations where political instability arises for one of the several reasons described earlier. However, it's my belief that a focus on building and sustaining trust in institutions—starting with the government but ultimately including the businesses that must keep an economy functioning—can independently prevent or exacerbate political instability experienced by a nation. In essence, *trust can and should be treated as a factor that is independently considered and managed*. Indeed, for a nation built on an ideal, the role of trust is particularly important to the U.S. system.

Countries that have a high risk of ultimate political instability can be expected to have low levels of trust throughout the society. Earlier we discussed the potentially disastrous consequences of failed reform efforts coinciding with previously high expectations. The rapid loss of confidence in the government, amidst failed expectations and reforms, leads to revolution or political instability. In this framework, the extent to which the government actively builds trust throughout the period of reform can serve as a powerful buffer to the negative emotions that accompany the collapse of rising expectations. If an unusually high degree of trust in government exists, despite the failure of reform, political instability is far more likely to be averted.

Why Trust Is So Important

Trust is a central component to political stability. All human societies depend on trust. At the most basic level, the green piece of paper we call a dollar has value only because each person trusts that he or she can trade it for something of value. In the fall of 2008, the financial system came near to collapse because the banks no longer trusted each other, and so stopped interbank lending. No bank knew whether other banks were holding toxic mortgages. In *Trust*, Francis Fukuyama demonstrated that societies with high trust are vibrant and productive because individuals trust that their interests will be protected.* In the absence of trust, rigid work rules, contracts, litigation, and a galaxy of other costs are created as everyone in the economy tries to protect him or herself. As trust breaks down, individuals typically adopt an "every man for himself" attitude rather than engage in productive activity or productive investments. In the complete absence of trust, the economy grinds to a halt.

Trust is a central element in any democracy. Citizens give up a certain amount of power over their own lives in

---

* Francis Fukuyama, *Trust: The Social Virtues and the Creation of Prosperity* (Free Press, 1995).

the belief that the government will act in their interests. Without trust, people become unwilling to cede power to government. Without trust, government itself eventually becomes ineffective, or provokes active conflict, as people lose confidence that leaders will be able to fulfill their responsibilities. Government statements come to be viewed as meaningless propaganda. In this extreme situation, government policies designed to promote the long-term health of the society are ignored as individuals worry about their own immediate well-being. The social fabric that holds the society together begins to unravel. This occurred in the late years of the Soviet Union when there was an extraordinarily high degree of cynicism toward the government. The government of Louis XVI was almost universally mistrusted before the French Revolution. At the time of the American Revolution the colonists lost trust in the British Parliament.

Trust and Economic Inequality

In *The Moral Foundations of Trust*, Eric M. Uslaner analyzed extensive data on the level of trust in the United States as well as other nations. His unambiguous finding was that trust in a society depends on the level of economic equality. Uslaner explains the results of his detailed statistical analysis by concluding, "Trust cannot thrive in an unequal world. People at the top will have no reason to trust those below them. Those at the top can enforce their will against people who have less . . . And those at the bottom have little reason to believe they will get a fair shake . . . The rich and the poor have little reason to believe that they share common values, and thus they might be wary of others' motives."[*]

Trust and Outcomes

We tend to think of trust as faith in particular individuals or institutions such as the president or Congress. Yet trust in the fairness of entire economic and political systems is also essential. A society must be true to its values. Americans admire people whose wealth is perceived to be fairly earned. When individuals amass huge fortunes without adding value to the society, however, there is often a sense of implicit corruption. It can seem that the system is biased in favor of these wealthy or powerful individuals. This can become one of the insidious side effects of economic inequality.

Similarly, when individuals lose faith that the system will treat them fairly, an important aspect of trust is lost. As the severity of the economic crisis increased—with the associated destruction of housing, equities, and pension assets—it created a question for many Americans that could have devastating consequences: Are hard work, sav-

---

[*]   Eric M. Uslaner, *The Moral Foundations of Trust* (Cambridge, 2002), 181.

ings, and an appropriately frugal lifestyle still rewarded? If not, can the basic economic system that governs our nation be trusted?

Trust as a Barometer of Revolutions

It may be possible for a government to manage trust despite failed policies or reforms. There may be ways of actively encouraging trust, through honest public statements. Total transparency can help create confidence that ultimately the problems that beset the nation will be solved—no matter what it takes. It has, for example, been argued that the United States avoided a revolution at the time of the Great Depression because of the unique relationship of trust FDR established with the American people. When leaders take positive steps to ensure that trust survives, even if policies fail, they are far more likely to move through periods of high risk with a nation intact. This is easier said than done. When a nation is in the grip of a severe trauma and policies to alleviate suffering have failed, it's a tall order for any leader to maintain the ongoing confidence and trust of his or her nation.

Returning to the five risk factors at the start of this chapter, the United States enjoys a terrific score in one category: the strength and history of its institutions. With the remaining four, however, there are serious causes for concern. How unequal are we? How much have our expectations been disappointed? How much could they be disappointed in the coming years? How unequal do we *perceive* ourselves to be? And finally, what sorts of shocks might hit? It is time to explore these questions in greater depth.

HOW UNEQUAL ARE WE?

AN OVERVIEW OF INCOME INEQUALITY

Since the late 1970s, America has been a terrific place to work for those at the top of the income structure. Unfortunately, the rest of the society has not shared this increased prosperity, and economic inequality has increased dramatically. It is not an exaggeration to say that, after accounting for inflation, the majority of working Americans have been waiting almost 30 years for a raise.*

---

* For example, Larry Summers, the former Harvard economics professor and president, and economic advisor to President Obama, found that the total gain in median family income in the United States adjusted for inflation between

Today, according to the most recent data, the United States is at the highest level of economic inequality in our nation's history. As noted earlier, since 1913 (when the modern federal income tax was instituted) income inequality in the United States has effectively followed a trend shaped like the letter U. Income inequality peaked in 1928 at the height of the Roaring Twenties, subsequently declined to form a trough from the start of World War II through the late 1970s, and has been steadily rising since then. In this chapter, we will look much more closely at the U to see how steep it really is.*

For starters, consider the share of income received by the top 10 percent of U.S. households. In 2006, the top 10 percent of U.S. households received incomes of $104,400 or greater, including both earned and capital gains income, according to the most widely accepted academic research.† In 1928, this top group of households accounted for just below 49.3 percent of the nation's total income. By 1944, the percent of total income held by this group declined substantially to about 33 percent and remained at this level until the 1970s. In the late 1970s the total income received by the top 10 percent of

---

1979 and 2004 was only 14 percent. Writing in 2007, Summers noted that 2004 reflected the most recent available data, but did not anticipate that the intervening years would have changed the results. Larry Summers, "Harness Market Forces to Share Prosperity," *Financial Times,* June 24, 2007.

* Saez, "Striking It Richer." The measure of income inequality used in this analysis is the percent of income received by the top 10 percent of U.S. families.

† The measurement of total household income in the United States is a complicated task. As a result, a number of different estimates exist. The Census Bureau uses a different methodology and puts this figure at approximately $136,000.

U.S. households began a steep ascent and reached an all-time high (thus far) of just above 49.3 percent in 2006.

Soon, it may well be that for the first time since we have kept recorded data, the top 10 percent of U.S. households will receive over 50 percent of the society's total income. This shift represents an unprecedented concentration of wealth.

Now, let's slice even more finely. Instead of the top 10 percent consider the top 1 percent—or 1 in every 100 families. Essentially, the trend is even more exaggerated. Income is concentrating in the hands of ever fewer numbers of people. In 2006, a household income of $376,400 or greater was the threshold for inclusion in this economically fortunate group. As a result of this ongoing shift toward greater inequality, the top 1 percent of Americans received almost 22.8 percent of all income in 2006, almost *one-quarter* of the total. The only time in which this percentage was higher was on the eve of the great stock market crash in 1928, when the top 1 percent of Americans received almost 24 percent of all income. By contrast, from 1952 to 1975 the top 1 percent received between 9 and 11 percent of total household income.

The Rise of the Super-Rich

Now, let's shift magnification one more time to look at the top 0.1 percent of American households, or 1 in every 1,000 families. Here, the increase in real income is the most dramatic. In 2006, the richest 0.1 percent of American families each earned $1,910,000 or more. Collectively this represented 11.6 percent of the total income earned by all U.S. households. In 1978, this group received a far lower 2.7 percent of total household incomes.

Here's one way to think about how much the top end of American income has increased as compared to everyone else. According to the Census Bureau, the median real income in the United States increased from a real income (measured in 2007 dollars) of $43,937 in 1978 to $49,568 in 2006: a gain of $5,631 or just 13 percent over 28 years. At the same time, the threshold levels for incomes of the top 1 percent of Americans (measured in 2006 dollars) increased from $198,100 in 1978 to $376,400 in 2006: a gain of 90 percent. As we move higher on the income scale, the difference becomes even more extraordinary. For the top 0.1 percent of Americans the threshold income (measured in 2006 dollars) increased from $566,800 in 1978 to $1,910,000 in 2006: a real income gain of $1.3 million, over 235 percent. While most of America has been waiting for a raise, the income at the top end of the spectrum has exploded.

All of the above data reflects pre-tax income and does not include government transfers (such as social security) or special benefits for the poorest citizens. However, these phenomena have minimal impact on the numbers, and do not change the basic trends or the conclusions that can be drawn from them.*

The great turning point was 1979. America in 1979 was a far more equal country than it is today. As noted earlier, the era starting at the end of World War II and continuing until the early 1970s has been called the "Golden Age" of economic equality in America. Consciously or inadvertently, that Golden Age was engineered through a combination of tax policies and social benefits. A large portion of the work force in the 1950s and 1960s was educated via the GI Bill. In 2006, Congress's Joint Economic Committee updated a cost-benefit analysis of this bill. In 2006 dollars, the GI Bill cost $51 billion. The Committee found that, in return, the GI participants created $260 billion in increased output relative to their less-educated peers, and an additional $93 billion in taxes.† The net return was seven dollars for every dollar invested. The GI Bill may be one of the greatest pieces of legislation ever enacted by our Congress. A century earlier, through the Lincoln-era Homestead Act, the Congress similarly gave every American the opportunity to start a new life in the West with free land, provided they lived on it and farmed it. Is there an equivalent opportunity for us to jump-start the opportunities and contributions of our citizens through legislation today? Let's hope so.

---

* With the exception of the data attributed to the Census Bureau, all of the data provided in this chapter up to this point is drawn from the Saez data described in the footnote on page 47. As noted earlier, the Saez data includes capital gains in calculating income.

† Humes, *Over Here*, 306.

• • •

Economists typically regard increased economic growth and increased productivity as two sides of the same coin, and the key to improved lifestyles. Productivity is the value in income (after adjusting for inflation) produced by each worker. Economists assume, reasonably, that when the economy grows, everyone shares in the benefits. Increases in productivity lead to rising living standards and wages. As output per worker grows, the nation becomes wealthier and the real incomes of workers rise.

From the late 1940s to the late 1970s, the share of incomes among different economic groups in America increased at approximately the same rate, which roughly reflected the nation's high gains in productivity. During this period, annual increases in GDP* closely matched the annual increases in median household income. As the nation became richer, all families benefited roughly equally. However, starting in the late 1970s these two elements began to diverge—income gains increasingly went to the highest earning Americans.† In effect, economic growth in the United States and increases in productivity have decoupled over the past 30 years. When

---

* GDP is the abbreviation for Gross Domestic Product, which is the total value of all final goods and services produced in a specific year in the nation.

† For a graphical representation of these trends, see Lane Kenworthy's blog Consider the Evidence, September 3, 2008, http://lanekenworthy.net/2008/09/03/slow-income-growth-for-middle-america/.

our economy has grown—a result of increased productivity—the benefits have only accrued to those at the top of the society.

Paul Krugman, Nobel laureate and Princeton economist, views the divergence between the growth in worker incomes and the growth in productivity with high concern. He notes that while the productivity of the average worker has increased by almost 50 percent since 1973, "the growing concentration of income in the hands of a small minority has proceeded so rapidly that we're not sure whether the typical American has gained *anything* from productivity."[*] If productivity gains had been widely shared across the work force, there is no question that the typical worker would be earning considerably higher wages today. The top of the society would have gained less, while the middle and bottom of the society would have done considerably better.

The distribution of wealth in the United States is even more skewed than the distribution of income. While most studies look at income as the best measure of inequality, wealth is perhaps more important. Wealth can be converted to income in times of need. It is a shield against bankruptcy in hard times. It has more influence on household spending patterns.[†] In a representative democracy,

---

[*]   Paul Krugman, *The Conscience of a Liberal* (Norton, 2007), 24
[†]   Edward N. Wolff, "Recent Trends in Household Wealth in the United States:

wealth can often be translated into the power to influence legislative decisions. The Task Force on Inequality and American Democracy, established by the American Political Science Association, for example, warned against the "subtle but potent threat" posed by "the growing concentration of the country's wealth and income in the hands of the few." The task force found that "Citizens with lower or moderate incomes speak with a whisper that is lost on the ears of inattentive government officials, while the advantaged roar with a clarity and consistency that policymakers readily hear and routinely follow."[*]

Edward Wolff of New York University, the nation's leading scholar of wealth trends, defines wealth as the sum of all liquid assets (including homes) less the sum of all debts (including mortgage debt). Wealth does not include guaranteed benefits, such as pensions or social security, since these cannot be marketed. In analyzing data through 2004, Professor Wolff finds that the top 20 percent of Americans own almost 85 percent of the nation's wealth.[†] Total wealth is even more concentrated as we move closer to the top. By 2004, the top 10 percent of households held 70 percent of all the nation's wealth, while the combined wealth of the top 1 percent of households was greater than the total wealth of

---

Rising Debt and the Middle Class Squeeze," Levy Economics Institute of Bard College, working paper no. 502 (June 2007), 2.

[*] *American Democracy in an Age of Rising Inequality*, Task Force on Inequality and American Democracy, American Political Science Association (2004), 1.

[†] Wolff, "Recent Trends in Household Wealth in the United States: Rising Debt and the Middle Class Squeeze."

the bottom 90 percent of households.[*] In the two decades proceeding 2004, the concentration of wealth in the United States increased, but not by an extraordinary amount.[†] For the most part, America's banana-republic-like wealth distribution has followed a set pattern since the 1980s.

To compare one society to another, economists use a statistical measure called the Gini coefficient. While the mathematics behind this calculation are somewhat daunting, it is a measure of the statistical dispersion of income among the population in a society. It is defined as a ratio that ranges between 0 and 1: The lower the Gini coefficient, the more equal the income distribution. A Gini coefficient of 0 equates to perfect economic equality (where everyone has precisely the same income), while a Gini coefficient of 1 equates to absolute inequality (where a single individual has all the income while everyone else has none). The UN-Habitat Monitoring and Research Division defines the Gini coefficient of .40 as an "international alert line," indicating that a society's "Inequality [is] approaching dangerously high levels" that could "lead to sporadic protests and riots."[‡]

---

[*]   U.S. Office of Management and Budget, *A New Era of Responsibility: Renewing America's Promise* (Section: Inheriting a Legacy of Misplaced Priorities) (February 2009), 9, http://www.whitehouse.gov/omb/assets/fy2010_new_era/Inheriting_a_Legacy1.pdf.

[†]   Wolff, "Recent Trends in Household Wealth in the United States: Rising Dept and the Middle Class Squeeze."

[‡]   UN-Habitat, *State of the World's Cities 2008/2009* (earthscan, 2008), 51.

• • •

I n 2007, the Census Bureau calculated that the U.S. Gini co-efficient stood at .463.[*] This measure is by far the highest measure for any industrialized nation. Economic inequality in the United States as compared to other industrialized nations is off the charts. An Organisation for Economic Co-operation and Development (OECD) study released in late 2008 found that of the 24 countries studied, the United States had the highest income inequality with the exception of Mexico and Turkey,[†] while a mid-2008 article in *Harvard Magazine* succinctly summarized the U.S. standing relative to other nations: "On the per capita GDP scale, our neighbors are Sweden, Switzerland and the U.K.; on the Gini scale our neighbors include Sri Lanka, Mali and Russia."[‡]

The United Nations Sounds An Alarm

It's often noted that the best observations about America are made by those who are not American. In this light, it's worth noting that a U.N. report voiced serious concerns with regard to the economic inequality in American cities.

---

[*] U.S. Census Bureau, *Income, Poverty, and Health Insurance Coverage in the United States: 2007*, August 2008, 7.

[†] BBC News, *More Inequality in Rich Nations*, October 21, 2008, http://news.bbc.co.uk/2/hi/business/7681435.stm.

[‡] Elizabeth Gudrais, "Unequal America: Causes and Consequences of the Wide and Growing—Gap Between Rich and Poor," *Harvard Magazine*, July–August 2008.

The *State of the World's Cities Report 2008/2009* found that the major U.S. cities with the highest levels of economic inequality included Atlanta, New Orleans, Washington, D.C., Miami, and New York. They face levels of inequality similar to such African and Latin American cities as Abidjan, Nairobi, Buenos Aires, and Santiago. Anna K. Tibaijuka, the U.N. under-secretary-general, notes that "urban inequality has a direct impact on all aspects of human development . . . In cities where special and social divisions are stark or extreme, lack of social mobility tends to reduce people's participation in the formal sector of the economy and their integration in society. This exacerbates insecurity and social unrest which, in turn, diverts public and private resources to . . . expenditures for safety and security."[*]

In effect, the U.N. report suggests that many U.S. cities have become gated communities where different classes of people exist without intermingling. The bonds that unite the larger nation as one community have weakened.

The Myth of American Mobility

Among Americans there is a general belief that our society is more mobile, more rich in opportunity than

---

[*]   UN-Habitat, *State of the World's Cities 2008/2009*, 2, 65.

old-world European societies. Social observers often claim that Americans tolerate greater inequality of economic outcomes in return for a greater shot at the brass ring. This is a central myth that defines America: the land of opportunity.

Do we put up with squalor amidst excess because we all have a shot at "making it"? In fact, our belief in mobility no longer has a basis in reality. Today, the best means of predicting the socioeconomic status of an individual in the United States is to look at the status of his or her parents.[*] Multiple studies have demonstrated that U.S. economic mobility is now substantially less than comparable mobility in European nations.[†] A startling study published in 2006 reviewed mobility patterns between the mid-1980s and mid-1990s and actually found that among the OECD countries the United States had the *lowest* share of low-income workers who change their status from one year to the next.[‡] Although this study reflects mobility patterns ending over a decade ago, a recent study undertaken for the Pew Charitable Trust concluded that there has been little, if any, change in mobility in the decades from 1984 to 1994 as compared to 1994 to 2004.[§]

---

[*] See George Irvin, *Super Rich: The Rise of Inequality in Britain and the United States* (Polity, 2008), 28.

[†] See, for example, Jo Blanden, Paul Gregg, and Stephen Machin, *Intergenerational Mobility in Europe and North America*, Centre for Economic Performance, London School of Economics, April 2005.

[‡] Irvin, *Super Rich*, 28.

[§] Gregory Acs and Seth Zimmerman, *U.S. Intergenerational Economic Mobility from 1984 to 2004: Trends and Implications*, Economic Mobility Project: An Initiative of the Pew Charitable Trust, 2008.

Americans have been willing to forego the European-style safety net, with guaranteed healthcare and typically greater vacation and pension benefits, in return for the perception of greater opportunity. We believe our business environment is the world's most dynamic. But if an overwhelming majority of us fails to benefit from that system or, worse, suffers misery and drastic reductions in our standard of living, how long will we continue to support it?

ECONOMIC INEQUALITY AND THE FINANCIAL CRISIS

The financial crisis destroyed a good deal of the world's wealth and jobs. Home values have plunged, and many savings plans for pensions and education have crashed. If anything, the crisis is a reason for even greater immediate concern about income inequality. Historically, economic downturns are particularly difficult for the middle class and the poor, who have fewer resources to weather the storm. The current downturn will exacerbate all of the tensions associated with economic inequality and add some new ones. The central question from the point of view of political stability is: how will it affect the middle class?

No one can predict the depth or severity of the economic crisis. Before the crisis, the finances of the American middle class were under severe pressure. Now, we run the real risk that the American middle class as we have always understood it will disappear. Harvard law professor Elizabeth Warren, who heads the Congressional Oversight Panel on the use of federal money in the government's first effort to bail out the banks (the Troubled Asset Relief Program or TARP),[*] is a leading expert on middle-class finances and the author or coauthor of several books on this topic, including *The Fragile Middle Class*.[†] She has voiced the possibility that, as a result of the financial crisis, "the middle class we once knew will disappear. America will move to a two-class economy—a substantial upper class that's financially secure and then a very large underclass that lives paycheck to paycheck."[‡] The consequences of these events for the stability of our political system would be catastrophic.

---

[*] The Congressional Oversight Panel was created as part of the Emergency Economic Stabilization Act of 2008 and is charged with reviewing the state of the financial markets and regulatory system and submitting regular reports to Congress. Elizabeth Warren is chairperson of the panel. See "TARP Oversight Panel Urges Transparency, Accountability," *Wall Street Journal*, January 10, 2009.

[†] Teresa A. Sullivan, Elizabeth Warren, and Jay Lawrence Westbrook, *The Fragile Middle Class: Americans in Debt* (Yale, 2000).

[‡] Kimberly Parker, "Elizabeth Warren: Middle Class Lacks Security" (interview with Elizabeth Warren), *U.S. News & World Report: Money & Business Blog*, February 9, 2009, http://www.usnews.com/blogs/alpha-consumer/2009/2/9/elizabeth-warren-middle-class-lacks-security.html.

ECONOMIC INEQUALITY AND THE MIDDLE CLASS

The middle class is notoriously hard to define. Jared Bernstein, the executive director of the Middle Class Task Force (a government-run investigative group), wrote on the Middle Class Task Force blog that the "Census Bureau tells us the median household income—the income of the household smack in the middle of the income scale—is about $50,000, so that's certainly got to be considered a middle class income."* But for some of us, "middle class" is in the eye of the beholder. A study by the Pew Research Center, *Inside the Middle Class: Bad Times Hit the Good Life*, released in April 2008, found that 53 percent of Americans say they are middle class. Of Americans with incomes less than $20,000, four in ten identified themselves as middle class, along with one-third of Americans with incomes above $150,000. Household size is also important. The Pew study defined a middle-class income as ranging between $45,000 and $89,000 in 2008 dollars for a household of three.† For a husband and wife with two children, these numbers would need to be larger. Location is also an important factor. One notable study argued that a person with an in-

---

* Jared Bernstein, executive director of the Middle Class Task Force and chief economist and economic policy advisor to the vice president, Middle Class Task Force blog, February 12, 2009, http://www.whitehouse.gov/blog/09/02/13/ What-is-the-middle-class/ (click on link to access Bernstein's discussion).

† Pew Research Center, *Inside the Middle Class: Bad Times Hit the Good Life*, April 9, 2008, http://pewsocialtrends.org/pubs/706/middle-class-poll.

come of $123,00 in New York City was middle class, while in Houston an income of $50,000 would qualify.*

To me, what matters is self-perception. And a great danger looms when the perception of "middle class" flips from one meaning "we're okay, we're moving up" to "we're losing ground." If the middle class feels that it is suffering at the expense of higher-income Americans, society is torn. When people who believe themselves to be middle class are not able to meet their expectations for a middle-class lifestyle, discontent spreads like wildfire. From this perspective, our focus will not be on defining the income of what makes someone middle class but on the increasing or decreasing ability of the broad swath of Americans who are below the highest income levels to afford what is typically seen as a middle-class lifestyle.

It is easy to identify what middle-class Americans have, over the last 30 years, come to anticipate as that lifestyle. As Bernstein writes: "It used to be that the middle class was able to achieve the American Dream of owning a decent home in a safe neighborhood with a good public school, having access to affordable health care, saving for college and retirement and enjoying the occasional meal out, movie, and vacation." These are the central factors—a home, access to healthcare, college for the kids, and retirement—together with job security or the ability to find a new, equivalent job relatively easily.

---

* See "N.Y.C. So Costly You Need to Earn Six Figures to Make Middle Class," *New York Daily News*, February 6, 2009 (reporting on a study released by the Center for an Urban Future).

As Bernstein notes, "The problem is that many middle class families are no longer able to afford this dream."[*]

In a nutshell, as wages stagnated over the past 30 years, the middle class financed its lifestyle through record levels of debt. As economic inequality has been rising in America, so has the level of debt compared to each family's available income. In the first quarter of 2008, total household debt was equal to 132 percent of personal disposable income. This represents an extraordinary increase from about 74 percent in 1979.[†]

As American debt increased, we stopped saving. Economists calculate that in 1981, personal spending represented about 88 percent of disposable income. By 2008, that number was roughly 100 percent. As a nation, our savings rate dropped from 12 percent to zero.[‡] (Since the beginning of the economic crisis, the savings rate has started to shoot back up, largely because of reduced availability of credit and more stringent lending standards.)

Middle-class families have borrowed heavily to hang onto their lifestyles. The costs of the basic building blocks of the middle-class lifestyle—housing, healthcare, and education—have been rising much faster than people's

[*]   Bernstein, Middle Class Task Force blog.

[†]   Christian Waller, *Economic Snapshot for September 2008*, Center for American Progress, September 9, 2008; Lawrence Mishell, Jared Bernstein, and Sylvia Allegretto, *The State of Working America 2006-2007*, Economic Policy Institute (Cornell, 2007) 271.

[‡]   Bureau of Economic Analysis, as detailed on Infectious Greed blog by Paul Kedrosky, *U.S. Savings Over Time: The Interactive Edition*, March 2, 2009, http://paul.kedrosky.com/archives/2009/03/us_savings_over.html.

median incomes. Now, as companies rescind credit lines and good jobs disappear, this thread is breaking.

High levels of middle-class debt are now coming due at a moment of fury: Families are facing the worst job market since the Great Depression, declining income opportunities, the elimination of credit options (as banks cut back on the availability of loans of all kinds), payments on homes with declining value often purchased during the housing bubble, increasing unemployment and thus decreasing access to affordable healthcare for many people, continuing increases in the costs of higher education, and drastically reduced liquidity and pension-related assets. The financial standing of many families may not survive this swarm of challenges, leading to an ominous downward economic cycle—what begins as a job loss or costly medical emergency turns into a crisis of foreclosure and ruined dreams.

The financial fragility of the middle class cannot be overstated. One recent study provided a snapshot of middle-class families in 2006. The study found that nearly *four out of five* middle-class families (78 percent) lack the basic financial security to weather the current economic downturn: They lack the net assets (defined as all assets except home equity less debt) to survive for even three months with spending at three-quarters of their current expense levels, should their source of income disappear.* A number of other studies support this conclusion, leading one press article to conclude "The results of a bevy of surveys found a growing number of consumers are only a couple paychecks away from a household collapse," and "A large number of households say that even one missed paycheck would spell financial ruin"† Too many of us have been living from paycheck to paycheck. Too many paychecks are coming to an end.

Assets are the shield that allows families to weather hard times, from unexpected financial bumps related to medical or other bills, to predictable bumps caused by college tuition. In the absence of meaningful assets, middle-class families are at the mercy of our increasingly unforgiving economy.

In the 1950s a high-end blue-collar worker could make ends meet on one salary, send the kids to college, and enjoy a modest annual vacation. This same worker could depend on his employer for health coverage and a viable pension when it came time for retirement. Today, families with two considerably higher white-collar incomes seem to have trouble meeting these same basic needs. Why? The answer lies in the skyrocketing costs of housing, healthcare,

---

*   Jennifer Wheary, Thomas M. Shapiro, and Tamara Draut, *By a Thread: The New Experience of America's Middle Class*, Demos and the Institute on Assets and Social Policy at Brandeis University, November 2007.

†   "Financial fears grow: More consumers are just a paycheck or two away from ruin," Marketwatch, March 20, 2009, http://www.marketwatch.com/news/story/Fears-grow-more-consumers-just/story.aspx?guid=(504D22FD-CC66-4FC1-BF8D-2F199C2AD042)&print=true&dist=printMidSection.

child care, and education. Elizabeth Warren and Amelia Tyagi describe the growing plight of many middle-income families in their definitive study, *The Two-Income Trap: Why Middle-Class Mothers & Fathers Are Going Broke.*

Warren and Tyagi conclude that in the 1950s, for a family with financial problems, Mom was the safety net: the stay-at-home mother could always go to work. By the early 2000s because of rising home prices and stagnant wages, two incomes were required to maintain the same middle-class lifestyle afforded by a single working dad in the 1970s or earlier. For families with preschool-age children, child care proved to be a large expense that often nearly erased the second earner's after-tax income. Warren and Tyagi write, "This bears repeating. Today after an average two income family makes its house payments, car payments, insurance payments, and child care payments, they have less money left over *even though they have a second, full-time earner in the workplace.*"[*]

For the middle class today there is effectively no safety net. Period. The social safety net of welfare, income assistance, and Medicare catches those at the bottom rung of our society. For everyone in the middle, the "net" is more like a nearly empty swimming pool. Unemployment insurance does not begin to match the typical middle-class wage. A laid-off middle-class worker is faced with increased healthcare costs (even if he or she elects COBRA

---

[*]   Elizabeth Warren and Amelia Warren Tyagi, *The Two-Income Trap: Why Middle-Class Mothers & Fathers Are Going Broke* (Basic, 2003), 51–52.

protection) and a dramatically reduced income. Since the early 2000s, few middle-class workers who lost their jobs found work with equal pay. In fact, between 2000 and 2007, real median income of households headed by those under 65 fell by an estimated $1,951.* While the economy expanded during this period, and productivity grew at 2.5 percent per year, both existing income and income gains shifted to those at the top of the society. The incomes of the middle and lower classes suffered even as the economy of the nation as a whole expanded.†

In our more difficult economic climate, it is impossible to anticipate that laid-off middle-class workers—many of whom have limited assets—will find jobs approaching their current income. Indeed, the difficulties associated with the current job market are captured in a monthly report released by the Bureau of Labor Statistics. In September 2008, the organization reported that there were 1.9 employees seeking work for every available job opening.

By April 2009, this ratio had increased to 5.4.‡ It's easy to see why a job loss today is a financially devastating event. It is one thing to identify the risks to the middle class. Predicting the future is, of course, something else entirely. If

---

* U.S. Office of Management and Budget, *Fiscal Year 2010* (February 2009), 8.

† Jared Bernstein, *Median income rose as did poverty in 2007; 2000s have been extremely weak for living standards of most households* (Economic Policy Institute Research: August 26, 2008), http://www.epi.org/publications/entry/webfeatures_econindicators_income_20080826/.

‡ Heidi Shierholz, *Less than one job opening for every five job seekers* (Economic Policy Institute: June 9, 2009), http://www.epi.org/publications/entry/jolts_20090609/.

I am correct, that we face a growing risk of the worst possible outcome—revolution—it is because the problems we face are so deep and fundamental that they cannot be easily fixed.

To assess the future, then, we need to understand the causes behind the inequality of the past three decades. Are they reversible? Or are we stuck in a trend that can only lead to disaster?

CHAPTER FIVE

WHY HAS INEQUALITY ESCALATED DRAMATICALLY?

INTRODUCTION

The extensive change in economic equality over the past 30 years has spawned an outpouring of different explanations. Economists, political scientists, policymakers, and sociologists on all sides of the political spectrum have advanced different theories to explain this vast change in the makeup of our society. These explanations have tended to focus on one or two broad areas within the economy, such as the increasing need for greater skills to succeed in the work force or the impact of globalization and foreign competition.

Yet we are attempting to explain a massive 30-year shift in the way Americans live and work, a fundamental realignment in the way our economy operates. My general perspective is that there is rarely a single simple explanation for a lasting trend of such mammoth proportions. It borders on the absurd to suggest that any one factor *could* influence the operations of the U.S. economy to this extent.

What actually happened was a fundamental shift in the philosophy underlying the way our economy operated. For lack of a better phrase, I call it "free-market exuberance." This philosophy led to a range of political actions, or a lack of actions (which can be just as significant), that created many different effects, each of which contributed to growing economic inequality.

THE PHILOSOPHY OF FREE-MARKET EXUBERANCE

Ronald Reagan launched the modern American reverence for free markets. Some of the manifestations of this philosophy included:

- a general assumption that public policy choices were unnecessary and often harmful, since markets always led to the best outcomes;
- a bias against regulation, as markets were assumed to be self-policing;

- an assumption that within a market economy there was no such thing as excess, since the market always correctly allocated resources;
- the firm embrace of the idea, incorrectly attributed to Adam Smith, that individuals who served their own ends within markets inevitably created a wealthier society (the doctrine of the "invisible hand" as a rationale for selfishness);
- and the repeated decision by top officials to ignore the potential that asset bubbles could arise with highly destructive impacts.

The philosophy of free-market exuberance was accompanied as well by an unabashed skepticism of government. When President Reagan declared in his first inaugural address that "government is the problem," he declared a policy of free-market exuberance, where unfettered markets were the solution. If market-based results were less than optimal, they were still presumed to be better than those that could be obtained through government intervention. In effect, Reaganites claimed, if the markets can't solve any problem, government can't either. Today, as citizens look to the government for assistance during a severe economic crisis, it's hard to laugh at Ronald Reagan's once-popular joke, "The nine most terrifying words in the English language are: 'I'm from the government and I'm here to help.'"

The components of free-market exuberance are worth discussing in some detail.

The Market as Morality

First, the outcomes of the market are assumed to be as necessarily better than active public policy choices. We no longer need to decide whether something is good or bad by debating it, since the market handles that decision for us. From this perspective, criticisms of economic inequality can be easily dismissed. Unequal wealth is the natural outcome of a market-based economy.

Yet, as we confront the most serious economic crisis in a century, it's already clear that an over-reliance on markets can lead to results that are detrimental to our entire society—even when individual participants are acting in their own best interests. The year 2008 may, perhaps, be recognized as the year we concluded that each person acting in his or her own interest *does not* necessarily lead to the best outcomes for society as a whole. The high returns available from high-risk derivative securities created incentives for individual investment bankers (acting in their best self-interest) to take risks that harmed the welfare of our entire society. Such activities can be viewed as a microcosm of the central concern of this book. We have established a social system that encourages each individual actor to rationally pursue results, no matter how selfish, that ultimately exacerbate economic inequality. The sum total of all of these individual actions, just like the creation and sale of financial derivatives, creates high risks for our society as a whole.

We must recognize that markets are created by people and nations to advance our mutual prosperity. We often treat markets as if they exist apart from politics or human creation. Yet, of course, each market is entirely a creation of our abstract imagination and designed to serve a particular goal. Markets exist because we decide to buy and sell things, following whatever rules we set. Desire is natural; markets are not—they are a social channeling of desire. For example, there is nothing natural about a market for patents. Our public policy channels inventive efforts by individuals in a specific way, determines how these efforts can achieve protection against competition (in the form of a patent), and then allows it to be sold in a "market." Calling markets natural is like calling marriages "natural." They may be inevitable, but they are still subject to collective decision making.

The Idea of the Invisible Hand

The research for this book began over three years ago. At the time, the almost universally held, positive view of unfettered markets was so strong that I assumed I would need to spend a great deal of energy demonstrating that markets—without appropriate rules and supervision—can hurt our overall society. Today, in the wake of the absolute failure of so many markets—ranging from the housing market, to the mortgage lending market, to the derivatives markets—such discussions are no longer necessary.

However, it is worth noting that the presumed intellectual grounding for the idea that the selfish pursuit of our own goals will, through the magic of the markets, lead to the best outcome for society is *incorrect*. This concept is attributed to Adam Smith, who wrote in *The Wealth of Nations* that when every individual works to promote his own well-being within a market, the net result, led by "an invisible hand," is the best possible result for society as a whole.

In fact, Smith did not intend to justify the single-minded pursuit of profits at any cost. In referring to the "invisible hand" Smith was not actually discussing markets. He was discussing why local inhabitants are good judges of local economic opportunities, as opposed to distant observers.[*] The oft-quoted phrase from Smith is actually a misquote, which omits his reference to "domestic industry." The correct quote is:

> By preferring the support of domestic to that of foreign industry, he intends only his own security; and by directing that industry in such a manner as its produce may be of the greatest value, he intends only his own gain, and he is in

---

[*] Jerry Z. Muller, *Adam Smith in His Time and Ours* (Princeton, 1993), 87.

this, as in many other cases, led by an invisible hand to promote an end which was no part of his intention.

Smith was actually arguing for domestic investment, as opposed to pure free trade.* It also seems unlikely that he considered this idea to be his seminal statement on markets since he did not include it in the section of *The Wealth of Nations* that actually addressed how markets function. In *Adam Smith's Lost Legacy*, Gavin Kennedy persuasively argues that Smith was actually referring to the *irony* of individuals acting in their own interests in very specific circumstances. Smith did not intend this phrase to say "anything about a general, let alone defining, trend in commercial society."† Smith wholly recognized the inherent failings of markets and the corresponding need for government vigilance. In fact, it's reasonable to assume that Smith would have argued against a whole-hearted endorsement of free-market exuberance, since Smith balances his praise of free markets with what commentators have called "an unapologetic realism about the limits of markets and the vital role of government in establishing, maintaining, defending, assisting, regulating, and supplementing them."‡

---

* See Jonathan Schlefer, "Today's Most Mischievous Quotation," *The Atlantic*, March 1998.
† Gavin Kennedy, *Adam Smith's Lost Legacy* (Palgrave Macmillan, 2005), 167.
‡ Lawrence D. Brown and Lawrence R. Jacobs, *The Private Abuse of the Public Interest: Market Myths and Policy Muddles*, Chicago Studies in American Politics

The Belief in Trickle-Down Economics and Associated Tax Cuts

One of the central tenets of economic policy over the past several decades has been the idea that as individuals become wealthy, their spending trickles down to benefit the other classes in society. According to this principle, massive concentrations of wealth could be regarded as a positive development. The new super-rich were the people whose spending would lift the rest of us.

The persistence of extreme economic inequality is testimony to the failure of this overarching principle. While real wages at the top of our economic strata have climbed into the stratosphere, wages have remained moribund for working families. Moreover, all but the most conservative economists now acknowledge central flaws in the free-market guiding philosophy.

As Paul Krugman wrote in the *New York Times*, "But it's not just trickle-down that has been refuted: the whole idea that a rising tide raises all boats, that growth in the economy necessarily translates into gains for the great majority of Americans, is belied by the Bush-era experience."[*]

(University of Chicago Press, 2008), 14.

[*] Paul Krugman, "Where's My Trickle?" *New York Times*, September 10, 2007.

Deregulation or *No Regulation* of Markets

A central aspect of free-market exuberance was the belief that government regulation was unnecessary. Rational actors would act responsibly or market forces would penalize them. As a consequence, the government repeatedly chose to weaken, eliminate, or avoid regulations for markets of all types.

A fundamental tenet of a well-functioning market is that all participants have equal access to information. The more information available within the market system, the better it performs. From this perspective, government has an important role to play, a role that *was* identified by Adam Smith: creating the appropriate "preconditions for the market."[*] If investors buy and sell derivatives without understanding their risks, the market is set up to fail. Only government regulation can help.

The philosophy of free-market exuberance, however, embraced an extreme view of government noninvolvement. In a well-known example, the Commodity Futures Modernization Act enacted under President Clinton exempted credit default swaps from regulation by the Commodity Futures Trading Commission. Disastrous consequences ensued. The lack of regulation and transparency in the markets for a range of derivatives (securities that are "derived" from the value of other financial instruments) was one of

---

[*]   Muller, *Adam Smith in His Time and Ours*, 87.

the factors that precipitated the economic crisis. Notably, Warren Buffett warned in 2003 that these highly complex financial instruments were a time bomb and "weapon of mass financial destruction" that could harm the whole economic system.[*] In a famous decision in favor of regulations that provide open processes, Supreme Court Justice Louis Brandeis wrote "Sunlight is the best disinfectant." Instead, our entire economy became infected by the darkness of unregulated derivatives.

Private markets, markets with lax enforcement, and deregulated markets all created opportunities for the accumulation of massive wealth by individual participants. Greater economic inequality was an inevitable result. Ironically, while the philosophy of free-market exuberance asserts the overwhelming efficiency of markets, the practical implementation of this philosophy actually led to far lower efficiency and far worse outcomes than a well-maintained, highly transparent system could have accomplished.

Bubbles Can't Exist

In an efficiently priced free market, there is no such thing as an asset bubble. The essence of the so-called efficient market hypothesis is that stock prices, or other efficiently priced assets, are *always* correctly priced because

---

[*] "Buffett Warns on Investment Time Bomb," *Economist*, March 4, 2003.

they reflect the sum total of investor knowledge about the future prospects for the value of the asset. This hypothesis is generally applied to stocks but the same reasoning applies to other large public markets, such as housing.

The experience of the dot-com boom in the 1990s and the extraordinary rise in housing prices in the 2000s, followed by the equally sharp drops in both markets, certainly suggests a strong disconnect between this theory and reality. Even if the hypothesis is normally true, it's clear that herd behavior and "irrational exuberance" can overwhelm otherwise rational pricing.* Many experts continue to believe that market prices are always best, except when they aren't. If this conventional wisdom seems flawed to you, you are not alone.

The Federal Reserve is generally the entity charged with seeing that the economy and markets don't overheat. The person most associated with the recent asset bubbles, however, is none other than former chairman of the Fed Alan Greenspan. Greenspan, who has now acknowledged the existence of a housing bubble, defends his legacy by saying that it's impossible to identify asset bubbles until they burst.†

Through interest rates, regulatory authority, and the force of the bully pulpit, Greenspan certainly had the abil-

---

* See Robert Shiller, *Irrational Exuberance*, 2nd ed. (Princeton, 2005).

† Peter Hartcher, *Bubble Man: Alan Greenspan and the Missing 7 Trillion Dollars* (Norton, 2006), 173–176; "Greenspan Admits Errors to Hostile House Panel," *Wall Street Journal*, October 24, 2008.

ity to tamp down the rapid, now obviously speculative rise in housing prices. There are two possible explanations for Greenspan's policies: He may have truly believed that market forces would regulate these mechanisms despite the evidence, which was obvious even then, that the country was in a speculative fervor. (Years later, he testified before the House Committee on Government Oversight and Reform that he was "in a state of shocked disbelief"[*] that the markets did not self-adjust.) Alternatively, whether consciously or not, he did not want to be the classic, dour central banker. As Paul Krugman writes, "Nobody likes a party pooper."[†] Greenspan liked being regarded as a genius who had brought wealth to all of America. As we now know, it was a false wealth, and a fundamental abrogation of the Federal Reserve's responsibilities.

For our purposes, the creation and destruction of asset bubbles are extremely important on two fronts: First, the assets that inflated in value, and then deflated, led—in themselves—to a tremendous transfer of wealth. In the dot-com bubble this transfer clearly moved from the mass of NASDAQ investors to a relatively small number of company founders, those who provided the initial financing for these companies, and to the employees of the Wall Street firms that took them public. Where the companies involved represented the creation of valuable new

---

[*] "Greenspan Concedes Error on Regulation," *New York Times*, October 23, 2008.

[†] Paul Krugman, "Lest We Forget," *New York Times*, November 27, 2008.

services, such as Amazon or eBay, few would begrudge the founders their handsome rewards. However, many individuals and financial services firms were enriched by selling stock in dot-com companies that were later deemed to be worthless.

The housing bubble was not as different as you might think. Some homeowners gained, but most did not: their gains were only on paper, or they sold high but had to buy higher. However, the transfer of wealth that occurred *in the services associated* with the housing bubble are very clear. The mortgage, debt, and financing mechanisms that created this asset bubble led to enormous (and with hindsight unwarranted) salaries in multiple financial services industries. Thus, asset bubbles became, in themselves, a mechanism for transferring wealth to the upper income strata of society.

THE EVOLVING ECONOMIC ENVIRONMENT

It would be irresponsible to suggest that the ethos of free-market exuberance bears sole responsibility for extreme economic inequality in the United States. Over the past three decades, our economy has confronted a variety of new forces, most notably globalization, fueled by the growing industrialization of nations such as South Korea, China, and India; and dramatic changes in technology with immense consequences for individuals, businesses, and the fate of entire industries. There is no doubt that these evolving forces also contributed to increased economic inequality in the United States.

Yet our response to all of these events has been filtered through the guiding ethos of free-market exuberance. For example, two economists at MIT, Frank Levy and Peter Temin, have focused on what they call the change in "institutional" arrangements that occurred after 1980.* They note that in the 1960s when U.S. Steel decided to raise prices by $6 per ton, President Kennedy called such increases "unjustifiable and irresponsible defiance of the public interest" and indicated that the government would not buy steel from the company. As a result, U.S. Steel backed down. In contrast, when the air traffic controllers union went on strike under President Reagan, he decertified the union. Levy and Temin argue that globalization, changes in technology, and all of the other forces that caused the growth of inequality took place within a framework of anti-regulation, anti-labor policies created by our government and supporting institutions. They suggest that rising economic inequality over the past 30 years may not have evolved if the institutional framework created by government had a different operating ethos.† We could have employed market incentives and explicit government policies to respond differently to the new business environment. Technological change and

---

*   Frank Levy and Peter Temin, *Inequality and Institutions in Twentieth Century America*, MIT working paper no. 07–17, revised June 27, 2007.

†   Ibid.

globalization were not brand-new ideas in 1980. During the Golden Age of Equality from the 1950s through the 1970s, technology changed, currency systems changed, and nations developed. It's the policy context surrounding these forces that explains the differences between the fifties and the nineties.

Nobel laureate Paul Samuelson perhaps put it best:

Based on my observations of economic history, both short run and long run, I believe that there is no satisfactory alternative to market systems as a way of organizing both economically poor and economically rich populations.

However, using markets is not the same thing as unregulated capitalism so beloved by libertarians. Such systems cannot regulate themselves, either micro-economically or macro-economically. Wherever tried they systematically breed intolerable inequalities. And instead of such inequality being the necessary price to encourage dynamic progress via technological and managerial innovations, it instead breeds dysfunctional shortfalls in what economists call "total factor productivity."[*]

---

[*]   Paul Samuelson, "The Dynamic Moving Center," *Der Spiegel*, November 12, 2008.

THE PROXIMATE CAUSES OF INEQUALITY

Free-market absolutism set the tone and governed our responses to every economic question raised since 1980. What were the most challenging of those questions?

1. Technology, Leverage, and Speculation

The PC revolution, from data processing to the Internet, fueled increased economic inequality. Companies could accomplish more with fewer people. The aggressive use of technology—typically anointed with the term "reengineering"—allowed businesses to eliminate layers of middle managers. At the same time, activities that previously involved some mix of repetitive work and skills were also gradually automated.

While workers in the middle ranks were often eliminated, top management was rewarded with higher salaries and increased stock options as increased profits reflected the benefits of new technologies.

A related aspect of technology is that it allows a few people to obtain leverage over a previously inconceivable volume of activities. Two clear examples where this had had an impact on incomes at the high end of the society are the Internet and finance-related businesses.

Over the past several years, we have seen the dramatic growth of hedge funds and other investment vehicles that control and invest large amounts of capital. Using sophisticated, often computer-generated trading strategies, these funds are now managing in excess of a trillion dollars,* *with limited manpower.* In the past, the management of money required a certain number of people simply to oversee all of the transactions, the execution and implementation of strategies, the development of investment opportunities, and possibly the clearance of legal or regulatory hurdles. As Wall Street increasingly became an investment bazaar, with any number of sophisticated products offered by investment banking houses, firms controlling investment capital could create programs that would execute investment strategies based on predetermined formulas. As a consequence, a few individuals could decide on an investment strategy and use technology to carry out a massive investment effort.

In combination with the use of technology, hedge funds were also able to convince investors that their expertise merited a pay scale similar to venture capital: They receive an annual management fee (typically 2 percent of funds under management) and 20 percent of all gains.

It was inevitable that some extraordinary winners would emerge. One example of this phenomenon is Paulson & Co., which anticipated the housing downturn and aggressively invested in investment vehicles that would profit when such a downturn occurred. As a consequence, John Paulson is believed to have personally earned $3.7 billion in 2007, and $2 billion in 2008. (And I remember when it used to take an entire career to earn just one billion!) And Paulson's

---

* "Hedge Funds Cut Down to Size," *Financial Times,* January 11, 2009.

compensation was not unique. Combined, the top 50 hedge-fund managers in 2007 personally earned $29 billion,[*] while in 2008, despite the downturn in the markets, the top 25 managers personally earned $11.6 billion.[†]

The investment banking houses similarly found that combining technology with sophisticated computer models allowed them to deploy large amounts of capital in trading operations. By borrowing a portion of the capital, the amounts involved could be increased even further. By the early 1990s these profits had become so significant that power in the executive suites at the investment banks shifted. Traders were running the show.[‡]

The transition of the investment banking business from one based on client advice to one based on short-term trading profits had a number of consequences. First, successful traders started to demand huge paychecks (a percent of their winnings) with the implicit threat that they would take their skills elsewhere. This fueled an enormous run-up in Wall Street salaries and contributed to the growth of the very rich or super-rich as a class, with attendant income inequality.

Second, as commentator Kevin Phillips has written, "the impact on the real economy has been pernicious, not least in the transformation of finance from patient capital to impatient speculation." Unfortunately, nations

---

[*] "Wall Street Winners Get Billion-Dollar Paydays," *New York Times*, April 16, 2008.

[†] "Top Hedge Fund Managers Do Well in a Down Year," *New York Times*, March 24, 2009 (discussing estimates by *Alpha* magazine).

[‡] Kevin Phillips, *Arrogant Capital* (Little, Brown, 1994), 105.

that allow themselves to get caught in speculative fervor almost always experience disaster. This repeating pattern can be seen from Spain in the sixteenth century (with an economy dependent on gold from the New World) to Holland (which got caught up in tulip mania in the seventeenth century) to the Roaring Twenties (when crowds gathered around the stock ticker tape at lunchtime). Phillips notes the interconnection between speculative excess, economic inequality, and political instability:

> They erode the living standards of the ordinary folk and destabilize governments unable to interpret the complex new political and economic universe. The great bulk of the profits invariably goes to a small elite able to harness and ride the new techniques, technologies, and opportunities. So it was in 1600 and in 1825—and so it appears to be again now.*

Phillips was writing in 1994 about trends in U.S. finance that were beginning to emerge. His prescience was unfortunately ignored by policymakers, and now the United States, together with the rest of the world, must face the inevitable, damaging consequences of an era of mass speculative excess.

A similar example of the way technology enables small groups of highly skilled individuals to leverage

---

* Ibid., 103–104.

their talents occurs on the Internet. For movie companies, blockbusters can be extremely profitable since there is effectively no added cost for each additional viewer. The primary costs associated with the movie are its production, actor salaries, and initial marketing. Similarly, successful Internet services have little additional costs associated with growing popularity.

Today, it's possible for an Internet service to be started by a small number of people and (because the Internet is almost ubiquitous) grow to become enormously popular, with a still-small staff. Then, if the site is sold or shares of the business are offered to the public, this small staff reaps enormous rewards. One example of such a site is YouTube, which was sold to Google for $1.65 billion and had a staff of just 65 people, which implies that each employee on average created value of $25.4 million.*

The rapid rise of the instant Internet or biotech company actually had a double impact on building the incomes of the wealthiest Americans. While technology supported the creation of these new ventures, the highly paid finance industry focused the investing public on owning a share of these new entities. As a consequence, from the venture capital industry, which financed these businesses, to the investment bankers who took companies public, to the Wall Street analysts that certified the viability of these businesses, enormous incomes were derived.

---

* "Google Has Acquired YouTube," *TechCrunch*, October 9, 2006.

2. Globalization Aided by Technology

Ultimately, globalization hit American workers with a one-two punch. It started with the Bud crowd (blue-collar workers) but moved up to the white-collar Starbucks customers.[*]

As foreign economies evolved, other countries developed the technical skills to create factories and manufacture products previously made in the United States. The far lower wage rates in countries such as South Korea or Mexico ultimately made such outsourcing a competitive necessity. From the perspective of the individual firm, they became trapped in a race to the bottom (to lower costs) with competitors. When Maytag closed its refrigerator factory in Galesburg, Illinois, in favor of operations in Mexico and South Korea, the company was, from its perspective, attempting to stay competitive with General Electric, Whirlpool, and Frigidaire, which were already manufacturing abroad. A Mexican worker at the new Maytag factory would be paid $2 per hour, as compared to the $15.14 per hour at the Galesburg factory.[†]

As many economists have noted, the impact of globalization is not simply the loss of jobs in the United States, but its downward impact on wages. American workers are either competing with lower-paid foreign counterparts to keep jobs in this country or competing with fellow coun-

---

[*]   This wonderful phrase appears in Steven Greenhouse, *The Big Squeeze: Tough Times for the American Worker* (Knopf, 2008), 203.

[†]   Ibid., 199–201.

trymen for the jobs that remain. As Paul Samuelson said, "If you don't believe [offshoring] changes the average wages in America, then you believe in the tooth fairy."*

As the capabilities of the Internet evolved, it became possible for outsourcing to move up the food chain. In essence, any skilled job that did not require a physical presence could be moved overseas to take advantage of lower labor costs. Radiologists in India now analyze X-rays for Massachusetts General and other hospitals. Engineers in Moscow replace Boeing workers in the United States, and far lower cost Indians trained in U.S. law perform tedious lawsuit discovery processes previously performed by American lawyers or paralegals.† Earlier in our history there was the great middle-class and upper-middle-class exodus to the suburbs. Now, there is the great exodus of middle- and upper-middle-class *jobs* across the globe.

Of course, globalization has helped lift millions of people across the globe out of poverty, and it is not a zero-sum game. Nonetheless, for the American workers affected, globalization has meant a painful loss in earning power and opportunity.

3. Takeovers and the Market for Corporate Control

If you are under 40, you may not realize that there was

---

*   Steve Lohr, "An Elder Challenges Outsourcing's Orthodoxy," *New York Times*, September 9, 2004; see also Paul Samuelson, "Why Ricardo and Mill Rebut and Confirm Arguments of Mainstream Economists Supporting Globalization," *Journal of Economic Perspectives* (Summer 2004).

†   Greenhouse, *The Big Squeeze*, 203.

a time when the word "takeover" was not a central part of the business lexicon. In the mid-1970s the idea of the hostile takeover, as a beneficial aspect of the business landscape, took hold. A number of academics lauded these activities as a way of disciplining underperforming managers.

The impact of this new market for corporate control on economic inequality, has, to date, been largely ignored. However, my analysis suggests that these activities set far-reaching ground rules that had implications for decades on the evolution of economic inequality.

Corporate raiders such as Carl Icahn and T. Boone Pickens were the precursors of one portion of today's super-rich. Suddenly, *Wall Street Journal* readers were learning about individuals creating large fortunes through financial manipulation as opposed to the creation of substantive products or services. In addition, the financing of takeovers led to a boom on Wall Street: Those at the top of this pyramid, such as junk bond pioneer Michael Milken, entered the category of the super-rich in their own right. Meanwhile the investment banking businesses of advising on hostile takeovers and defenses, creating junk bonds to finance these deals, and selling the junk bonds led to a growing class of Wall Street wealth.

This represented, in part, the ascendance of Wall Street over Main Street. With the creation of the market for corporate control, Wall Street forever changed its relationship with corporate America: A new element of fear entered the relationship between Main Street (the source of prey) and Wall Street (the force behind each predator).

Additionally, the boom in reengineering, cost cutting, slimming down, and eliminating layers of middle management were all accelerated by management's belief that if it did not cut its own costs, a takeover would do it for them. In this regard, takeovers were a primary accelerator of the destruction of the long-lasting social contract between corporations and employees, which had previously worked to establish job security, benefits, and a living wage to longtime employees.

Finally, takeovers led to a new focus on the contracts of upper management—leading to golden parachutes and a greater focus on stock options. Although management stock options are generally seen as an innovation that aligned the interests of management with that of shareholders, they were also a means for top management to ensure that in the event of a takeover they would be extraordinarily well-compensated. A large class of very wealthy individuals was created by this takeover boom.

4. The Age of Excess: Executive Salaries

In 2007, the Associated Press (AP) estimated that the average pay package for the CEOs of S&P 500 companies was around $10.8 million, which is 270 times the average compensation of full-time nonmanagerial workers (roughly $40,000 including benefits).* Thirty years ago,

---

* "CEO Pay 364 Times More Than Workers," CNN Money.com, August 29, 2007, http://money.cnn.com/2007/08/28/news/economy/ceo_pay_workers/index. htm.

CEO pay averaged about 40 times the paycheck of the typical American worker.* While the real wages of median income families (those in the middle) have barely increased since 1980, average CEO compensation has skyrocketed.

We now live in an age of excess and it has become socially acceptable, even status enhancing, for CEOs to extract as large an income as possible. In the 1950s, a CEO would have been embarrassed to earn almost 300 times the wages of the typical worker. Any such embarrassment has long since left the executive suite.

When the trend toward higher CEO pay began, then Harvard Business School professor Michael Jensen was among its most outspoken proponents. Jensen argued that large packages appropriately reflected pay for performance. Yet today even Jensen is a critic of current pay scales. According to the *New York Times*, Jensen "is trying to find ways to fix the flaws that, in his evolving view, often allow mediocre chief executives—even outright failures—to become fabulously rich." "There are all kinds of mistakes, and we can do a lot better," Jensen told the paper. Jensen added that, "My way of characterizing the major thing that's wrong with large public corporations in the United States: the C.E.O. has no boss."†

While the press has focused on CEOs' salaries, other

---

* See John C. Bogle, *The Battle for the Soul of Capitalism* (Yale, 2005), 17.

† Louis Uchitelle, "Revising a Boardroom Legacy," *New York Times,* September 28, 2007.

high company officials similarly started seeking—and receiving—far larger compensation packages. Thus, while reengineering, globalization, and technology have decimated the ranks of middle managers, compensation trends have enhanced top executive compensation and created far larger gaps between top executives and everyone else.

5. Public Policy (tax policy, deregulation, unions, and "bubbles")

The political and economic ideology of free-market exuberance led to a vast range of initiatives that fostered the growth of extreme economic inequality. These ranged from tax policies, to regulatory policy, to an anti-union bias, to revisions of the bankruptcy code. The details of these initiatives could easily fill an entire book. Here is a brief overview:

Personal Income and Capital Gains Taxes

When Dwight Eisenhower took office, the top marginal tax rate for individuals was 92 percent. Under Ronald Reagan, these rates were reduced from 69 percent when he entered office to 28 percent by 1988. In 1993, the top tax on capital gains, for items held for more than one year, was dropped to 28 percent, then 20 percent in 1997, and then 15 percent under George W. Bush.

The lower capital gains rate provides tremendous value to hedge fund operators, venture capitalists, and private equity firms. The IRS reports that in 2006 the effective tax rate (the rate at which people actually pay taxes as opposed to the top ordinary income rates) for the top earning 400 Americans, those with reported incomes of *$263 million or more*, was a shockingly low 17.2 percent. This was the lowest rate in the 15 years the IRS has tracked the data.* Since the top 20 percent of society own 85 percent of its wealth, this lower capital gains rate also clearly benefited the wealthy at the expense of everyone else. Warren Buffett quips that if you take payroll taxes into consideration, these top earners pay lower tax rates than their receptionists. In fact, Buffett isn't joking. In 2006, he paid 17.7 percent of his taxable income, which exceded $46 million in taxes. His receptionist paid about 30 percent.†

One of the fascinating and horrifying aspects of our current system is that the highest paid people in the nation are, by and large, hedge-fund operators, some of whom personally derive annual incomes in excess of $1 billion by correctly betting on the movement of securities prices in specific markets. Their staffers are similarly well-compensated. There is nothing illegal about these activities, but they do strongly suggest that there is something wrong with our society. Figuring out how to arbitrage our markets is hardly the best use of talent in the nation. In theory, capi-

---

* "For 'Fortunate 400,' A Tumbling Tax Rate," *Wall Street Journal*, January 30, 2009.

† "Buffett Slams Tax System Disparities," *Washington Post*, June 27, 2007.

talism should allocate talent through pay structures to the most valuable uses. I will go out on a limb here: The activities of hedge-fund operators—while perfectly legal and to be expected—*are among the least socially valuable activities.* Yet their pay scales are now so high that they dwarf even those of publicly traded finance companies. Hedge-fund salaries make careers in anything that actually produces anything or solves any societal problem seem almost demeaning.

To add insult to injury, although the business of these funds is a professional service—the management of money—hedge-fund principals have been taxed at a capital gains rate through 2008 under what is known as the "carried interest rule" (when these rates apply to the investments of their funds). The activities of hedge funds have nothing to do with capital formation (the ostensible purpose of the capital gains rate) and should therefore be taxed at ordinary income levels. The first budget President Obama submitted to Congress included this change. With millions of suffering Americans, I would suggest that such reform now has an essentially symbolic value.

The tax cuts enacted under George W. Bush are particularly noteworthy. As Larry Bartels of Princeton University writes in *Unequal Democracy: The Political Economy of the New Gilded Age,* "the most significant domestic policy initiative of the past decade has been a massive government-engineered transfer of additional wealth from the lower and middle classes to the rich in the form of substantial reductions in federal income taxes." Many of the provisions of the tax cuts, such as reductions in dividends, the capital gains rate, and estate taxes, disproportionately benefited wealthy taxpayers. Bartels cites projections by the Institute on Taxation and Economic Policy that the total federal tax burden in 2010 "will decline by 25% for the richest 1% of taxpayers and by 21% for the next richest 4%, but by only 10% for taxpayers in the bottom 95% of the income distribution."[*]

In fact, the unanimous finding of all but the most conservative economists is that the Bush tax cuts solidly and unambiguously benefited the wealthy far more than other classes.

The Estate Tax

A central example of Bush-era free-market exuberance is the estate tax. Prior to the election of Bush, the federal estate tax stood at 55 percent on estates over $675,000, giving married couples the ability to leave $1.3 million to their children tax free. Bush proposed removing the tax altogether. The compromise legislation that was ultimately enacted increased the size of the exemption to $3.5 million in 2009, and reduced the tax rate to 45 percent. The legislation set out a schedule that culminates in 2010, when no estate tax will be assessed. The following year, 2011, brings back the 55 percent rate at a threshold of $1 million. In short, rich

---

[*] Larry Bartels, *Unequal Democracy: The Political Economy of the New Gilded Age* (Princeton, 2008), 161–162.

parents and grandparents should plan to die in 2010. (Nobody expects this ridiculous law to remain untouched.)

There are several striking aspects of the estate tax fight. First, there was no economic rationale for removing the tax in the first place. President Bush argued that it was necessary to save family farms and small businesses. In fact, earlier legislation had already accomplished this objective by granting a far larger estate tax exemption to small businesses. In selling the estate tax repeal, President Bush said, "to keep farms in the family we are going to get rid of the death tax." Soon, both the White House and the American Farm Bureau Federation (AFBF) were asked to identify families who had lost their farms as a result of the estate tax. Neither the White House nor the AFBF was able to identify a single family.[*]

Second, the estate tax has enormous symbolic meaning. A central aspect of the ideal of equality in America is the notion that our country is not dominated by a landed gentry. The estate tax guards against a permanent aristocracy of wealth.

The desire to eliminate the estate tax displays an extraordinary selfishness and arrogance on the part of the super-rich. When our wealthiest citizens support the total elimination of the estate tax, they signal that they owe nothing to society. They are in effect saying "I deserve every penny, and it's my right to give my heirs

---

[*]   David Cay Johnston, *Perfectly Legal* (Portfolio, 2003), 73.

a head start." That attitude, all by itself, is a potential threat to our democracy.

Regulatory Policy

The past 30 years have been marked by a stream of deregulatory efforts. Some of the most notable efforts included the elimination of the Glass-Steagall Act, which separated commercial and investment banks, the decision by the SEC in 2004 to allow five investment banks (Merrill Lynch, Morgan Stanley, Goldman Sachs, Bear Stearns, and Lehman Brothers[*]) to change the limit on their debt-to-net capital ratio from 12 to 1 to what was effectively between 30 to 1 and 40 to 1,[†] and the Commodity Futures Modernization Act, which prevented the regulation of the derivatives markets. The SEC decision to reduce capital reserves and the failure to regulate derivatives had the same effect: They encouraged financial institutions (including investment banks, other types of banks that bought and sold derivatives, insurers such as AIG, and hedge funds) to make risky bets, often based on high leverage. Some of these bets were successful, which made the individuals at these institutions fabulously wealthy. Others have been disastrous,

---

[*] Note: It is certainly not a coincidence that none of the banks that received authorization for this high-risk activity exists today in its former form.

[†] "Ex-SEC Official Blames Agency for Blow-Up of Broker-Dealers," *New York Sun*, September 18, 2008; "Agency's '04 Rule Let Banks Pile Up New Debt," *New York Times*, October 2, 2008.

leading to a devastating economic crisis. The longer-term impact may well be political instability.

Asset Bubbles

The housing bubble played a central role in exacerbating economic inequality and in creating the economic crisis. The important points here are that the Federal Reserve brought interest rates to a then historic low of 1 percent in June 2003, which pushed mortgage rates down and encouraged further speculation in the housing market. In 2004 and 2005, Alan Greenspan, the chairman of the Federal Reserve, was actively promoting alternatives to fixed mortgages as well as subprime lending.* None of the agencies evaluating banking stability or risk appeared to be concerned about the possibility that rising housing prices were really a gigantic credit bubble that would cause untold damage if they started to decline.

Within this frothy framework, a host of entities found ways to tap new sources of capital for the mortgage sector, largely by securitizing mortgages and turning them into investment vehicles. These activities, together with surrounding services and related trading bets, made it "normal" in many financial services companies for individuals to earn million-dollar paychecks. A system that

---

* William A. Fleckenstein with Frederick Sheehan, *Greenspan's Bubbles: The Age of Ignorance at the Federal Reserve* (McGraw Hill, 2008), 155–160.

effectively transferred wealth from "the masses" to an elite few was in full force.

Unions

By the mid-1950s, 35 percent of American workers belonged to unions. Today, just 7.5 percent of private sector workers, and 12.1 percent of all American workers, are in unions. Until the early 1980s, American corporations generally saw unions as "a sometime partner, sometime antagonist that they had to deal with, however reluctantly."[*] But under Reagan, attitudes shifted and corporate executives concluded that they could engage in all-out battles to defeat unions. President Reagan's firing of the illegally striking air traffic controllers helped turn anti-union activity into an act of patriotism.[†]

There is no question that unions failed to adapt to a changing world. In some cases, they became inflexible and ineffective. At the same time, we do need to recognize that union employees remain better paid, more secure, and far more likely to hang on to essential benefits such as health insurance and pensions than their non-union counterparts. Moreover, economic inequality was far less severe when unions were ensuring that the profit

---

[*] Greenhouse, *The Big Squeeze*, 243–247.

[†] Ibid., 247, quoting Martin Jay Leavitt and Terry Conrow, *Confessions of a Union Buster* (Crown, 1993), 247.

pie was more equitably divided among all of a company's employees.

I do not profess sufficient expertise to know whether unions are ultimately good or bad for the economy. What I do know is that with no countervailing force, the business and financial sectors have created levels of wealth inequality—and an economy in such ruins—that the future of our political stability is at issue. Countervailing forces, whether it is unions in their current form, in a different form, or entirely different types of entities, are clearly needed. The long-term health of our political system may well depend on it.

CHAPTER SIX

THE INDICATORS ARE BLINKING RED

I
n early 2009, the idea that the growing economic crisis might cause political turmoil was clearly in the minds of serious political observers across the globe—but not in the United States. *Foreign Policy* magazine considered whether the darkening economic horizon might lead to political instability in Putin's Russia.[*] An article in the online version of *Foreign Affairs* discussed whether the worsening financial crisis could destabilize China's political structure.[†] Numerous publications described the growing political and economic crisis in the Ukraine. At the same time, the head of the IMF warned that the global financial crisis could have serious implications for the political stability of the world's

---

[*]   Arkady Ostrovsky, "Reversal of Fortune," *Foreign Policy,* March/April 2009.

[†]   Minxin Pei, "Will the Chinese Communist Party Survive the Crisis?" Foreign Affairs.com, March 12, 2009, http://www.foreignaffairs.com/articles/64862/minxin-pei/will-the-chinese-communist-party-survive-the-crisis?page=show.

20 poorest nations.* Meanwhile investors voted with their wallets, and declared the United States the safest place on earth. One early consequence of the economic crisis was the historically low rate of interest on U.S. Treasury bills. In some cases, late in 2008, U.S. Treasury bills were actually paying negative interest. Investors were so concerned about finding a safe haven for their money that, in effect, they were willing to pay for the privilege of lending it to the U.S. Treasury. In an extraordinarily uncertain world, the U.S. government is seen as the most stable of all entities.

Although the world faces an economic emergency the likes of which few alive have ever experienced, the general assumption is that the United States is solid as a rock. Democracies, and in particular the United States, are presumed to be self-correcting: necessary change occurs through the ballot box. With the election of Barack Obama, many believe that such a self-correction has already occurred. America has elected its first black president, provided his party with a rare, solid majority in both houses, and the population, approving of the new president by 80 percent, appears to believe that the nation has turned a corner.

The nation entered the Obama era like a patient who had finally located the doctor who could heal her painful wounds. Amidst this extraordinary hope, from

---

* See, *IMF Calls for Urgent Action as Third Wave of Global Crisis Hits Poorest Countries*, IMF press release, March 3, 2009, http://www.imf.org/external/np/sec/pr/2009/pr0953.htm.

an extraordinarily optimistic people, within the longest lasting democracy in history, how can I seriously suggest that our democracy is at risk? For starters, the evidence of past instances of political instability must serve as a warning. We are at a particularly dangerous moment. We must recognize that the stakes associated with the success of the new presidential administration today are far higher than anyone has generally acknowledged. Hopes are so high precisely because our challenges are severe. If President Obama does not succeed, the disappointment will be extreme. And yet, the challenge of unbridgeable inequality is one that Washington cannot easily solve. We have already listed the causes of revolution, including inequality. Now it is time to apply these causes to the situation in the United States. Like a barometer, they can show the growing risk to our society as each condition is met.

OUR TROUBLED TIMES

Professional historians are often the most skeptical practitioners of the art of taking events in the past and imputing their meaning for the future. As the Durants wrote in *The Lessons of History*, "History smiles at all attempts to force its flow into theoretical patterns or logical grooves; it plays havoc with our generalizations, breaks all our rules; history is baroque." They concluded that "We must operate with partial knowledge and be provisionally content with probabilities; in history, as in science and politics, relativity rules, and all formulas should be suspect."*

One reason to study history is to recognize the *broad* patterns, as opposed to specific analogues, that predictably recur. As Arthur Schlesinger, Jr., puts it, the study of history is a valuable public policy tool "because generalization, sufficiently multiplied and interlaced, can generate insight into the shape of things to come." The point of the exercise is to find what Schlesinger calls the "variety of uniformities and recurrences," which can "strengthen the capacity of statesmen to deal with the future."†

A look at this list suggests that certain factors happen first: These might be labeled preconditions for a revolution. They are necessary but not sufficient. The three most common preconditions that precede political instability are *extreme economic inequality; an unexpected, significant major economic or political shock; and a long-suffering middle class.*

These circumstances set the stage. The next ingredients describe how a government and its citizens react to them. Once the need for action arises, it is the way in which this action is successfully or unsuccessfully implemented that ultimately determines the political stability of the nation.

Thus there are two phases to existential political crises.

---

*   Will and Ariel Durant, *The Lessons of History*, 13.
†   Arthur M. Schlesinger, Jr., *War and the American Presidency* (Norton, 2005), 124–125.

PHASE ONE: PRECONDITIONS

- Extreme economic inequality
- Severe economic shock affecting all aspects of the society
- A weak middle class
- A trigger of conflict (riots, coup d'état, terrorist strike, etc.)

PHASE TWO: RESPONSES

- The Middle Class
  * Degree of feelings of relative deprivation ("We are suffering for the greed of the rich") and level of associated anger
  * Post-shock expectations and ultimate outcome (degree of rising expectations followed by success or failure)
  * Perception of competence and fairness in government

- The Government
  * Ability to act
  * Ability to restore trust in the economic systems of the society
  * Ability to articulate believable hope for the middle class
  * Willingness to use force to maintain power

In the more than 200 years since the American Revolution, we have faced existential crises three times: the Civil War, the Great Depression, and now. The preconditions are almost all in place. We face historic levels of economic inequality. We have suffered an economic shock whose full consequences are not yet known. Finally, our vitally important middle class is perilously weak. What would happen if a trigger were set off?

We are an optimistic people. Our loyalty to our Constitution has withstood the strains of sectionalism (barely), the Depression (with some adjustments, notably in the powers of the federal government), and the war on terror (with some concessions). Revolutions generally do not occur in nations with long-established traditions of democracy.

Yet our very own loyalty to our traditions might set the stage for supreme disappointment. If the middle class was to conclude that the nation was no longer the United States of our ideals, expectations, and beliefs, it might rebel to reclaim that vision. As Jefferson noted in the Declaration of Independence, people have an inherent right to civil disobedience in the face of perceived tyranny.

The question is, when does inequality lead to tyranny? There are few greater blows to the spirit than the loss of one's home. Home ownership is central to the American Dream, encompassing the place of most families in a community, and a general sense of security—no matter how bad the job market or pension portfolio. The traumatic loss of a home is also a very public shame that inevitably leads to anger and despair. According to the

Census Bureau, there are approximately 76 million homeowners in the United States.* In 2008, more than two million homeowners faced foreclosure proceedings, and by the end of the year more than 11 percent of all mortgages were either delinquent by one month or in foreclosure.† Economists project that as many as eight to ten million families could lose their homes to foreclosure in the coming years, depending on the severity of the economic downturn and the success of government and private efforts to stem foreclosures.‡ If this is allowed to happen, it means as many as one in every eight homeowners in the entire nation will experience this public degradation.§ What level of anger, sense of failed expectations, and sense of unfairness would this create?

Civil disobedience can emerge, even among the most conservative and normally upright citizens. During the Great Depression, foreclosed farms were auctioned on local courthouse steps. As the situation worsened, farmers took matters into their own hands. In what became known as "penny auctions," neighbors of bankrupt

---

* U.S. Census Bureau, *American Housing Survey for the United States: 2007* (current housing reports), September 2008, http://www.census.gov/prod/2008pubs/h150–07.pdf.

† Mortage Bankers Association, *Delinquencies Continue to Climb in Latest MBA National Delinquency Survey,* press release, March 5, 2009, http://www.mortgage-bankers.org/NewsandMedia/PressCenter/68008.htm ("11.13 percent on a seasonally adjusted basis and 11.93 percent on a non-seasonally adjusted basis.")

‡ See Associated Press, "Foreclosures Fall from December to January," NYTimes.com, February 11, 2009.

§ Note: This calculation does not distinguish between foreclosures of homes that are owner-occupied versus rented.

farmers would gather for an auction, physically prevent people from bidding on foreclosed farms, and then bid a token amount for the farms with the goal of returning the homesteads to their original, foreclosed owners.* Moreover, to prevent additional foreclosures, farmers rioted in Iowa, threatened to march on the statehouse in Nebraska, and unleashed acts of violence across the Midwest.† "The West is seething with unrest," said FDR.‡

These generally conservative farmers viewed their rebellion within the context of American principles. Arthur Schlesinger, Jr., who published the three-volume study *The Age of Roosevelt*, wrote, "Theirs, as they saw it, was the way not of revolution but of patriotism." As one elderly farmer who participated in a blockade of Sioux City put it, "They say blockading the highway's illegal. I says, 'Seems to me there was a Tea-party in Boston that was illegal too.'"§

I have no doubt that these farmers would have explained their actions as a combination of anger and righteousness that would be echoed in our modern era: A corrupt system of home loans, combined with an economic system that was run for the benefit of a privileged few, unfairly destroyed their lives. In the face of such blatant corruption of the American ideal, and the absence of a sense of shared suffering by everyone in the nation, the

---

*   Robert S. McElvaine, *The Great Depression: America, 1929–1941* (Random House, 1984), 135; David M. Kennedy, *Freedom from Fear,* 196.

†   Manchester, *The Glory and the Dream,* 58–59.

‡   Kennedy, *Freedom from Fear,* 196.

§   McElvaine, *The Great Depression,* 91–92.

farmers' actions seemed justified. What could law enforcement do today if faced with something similar?

It's not impossible that a bedraggled middle class, which has suffered through ever-diminishing job prospects, pension losses, declining mobility, and stock losses caused by the nation's elite, would forcefully reject massive home foreclosures today. A harbinger of things to come may well be the civil disobedience program, launched in early 2009, by Acorn, a community activist organization. The program calls for volunteers in at least 22 cities to join evicted homeowners in refusing to leave foreclosed properties, and risk jail if necessary. In describing the program, the *New York Times* noted, "In recent months, a budding resistance movement has grown among Americans who believe they have been left to face their predicament on their own—and the Acorn campaign is an organized expression of that frustration, Ms. Lewis [Acorn's chief organizer] said. Instead of quietly packing up and turning their homes over to banks, homeowners are now fighting back." A central element of this rising anger and frustration will be the extent to which people across the income spectrum believe that the government has effectively abandoned them to their fate. These emotions are captured in Ms. Lewis's statement, "these families are now saying enough is enough."[*]

As this book goes to press, the federal government

---

[*] "Effort Takes Shape to Support Families Facing Foreclosure," *New York Times*, February 17, 2009.

has guaranteed trillions of dollars in loans to financial institutions, yet virtually nothing to help the victims of foreclosure. And the foreclosure problem is only one of several ways in which the economic crisis, if it deepens, could lead formerly law-abiding citizens to decide that the laws have been rigged against them. Consider unemployment. If job losses continue at an ominous pace, all kinds of misery, loss of status, and public indignation will result.

The rule of law holds only to the degree the law seems fair. Already today there is a proliferation of groups in several cities that settle homeless people into bank-owned but empty foreclosed properties. The idea that thousands of homes are sitting idle, while an increasing number of dispossessed Americans lack shelter, strikes many people as fundamentally unfair. And the police look the other way, effectively conspiring to break the law to "fix" the problem.* This behavior, which is effectively civil disobedience on the part of the police, may be a harbinger of things to come.

The idea that extreme economic inequality causes panics, depressions, and economic meltdowns has received little to no attention from mainstream econo-

---

* See "Homeless Turn Foreclosures into Shelters," *USA Today*, December 11, 2008; Democracy Now, "Take Back the Land: Miami Grassroots Group Moves Struggling Families into Vacant Homes," Amy Goodman interview with Max Rameau, Miami-based organizer with Take Back the Land, December 19, 2008, http://www.democracynow.org/2008/12/19/take_back_the_land_miami_grassroots.

mists, with one glaring exception. In his seminal work *The Great Crash, 1929,* John Kenneth Galbraith lists the five "weaknesses" that had the greatest impact in causing the disaster. The first item on this list is "The bad distribution of income in 1929," which he estimates allowed the top 5 percent of the population to receive one-third of all personal income. Galbraith asserts that this "unequal income distribution" made the economy overly dependent on both "investment in new plants and new projects" and "a high level of luxury spending" or both, since "the rich cannot buy great quantities of bread." He concludes that both investment and luxury spending are "inevitably" more "erratic" and subject to "wider fluctuations" than "the bread and rent outlays of the $25-a-week workman. This high bracket spending and investment was especially susceptible, one may assume, to the crushing news from the stock market in October of 1929."[*]

Now, we can add the Crash of '08 to the evidence that was not available to Galbraith when he studied the Great Depression. Indeed, it seems almost impossible to assert that there is no relationship between economic disaster and extreme economic inequality when the two greatest economic disasters in the past 100 years *immediately followed the only two periods of extreme economic inequality* during this same period.

---

[*] John Kenneth Galbraith, *The Great Crash, 1929* (Houghton Mifflin, 1954), 177–178.

Nonetheless, there have been almost no voices among modern-day economists who suggest the economic meltdown that occurred in late 2008 was related to economic inequality. One notable exception is the Nobel laureate Joseph Stiglitz. He asserts that because of an "insufficiency of global aggregate demand" the Federal Reserve pursued economic policies that inevitably played a central role in causing the crash. As Stiglitz tells the story, rising economic inequality "transferred money from people who would spend it to people who don't spend it." As a consequence, to maintain our economy we "tried to get around the problem" by saying to those lower on the income scale "don't worry you can continue to spend as if you had income, " and "encouraged them to go into debt finance." Our household savings rate fell to zero, and the entire structure "was clearly not sustainable." Eventually, the inability of our debt-burdened society to keep spending led the system to crash. He is now concerned that as we attempt to manage the crisis, "We aren't paying attention to some of the underlying causes that got us into the problem."[*]

I believe that extreme economic inequality and a poorly functioning economy are mutually reinforcing. Our nation operates in a highly competitive economic environment where highly competitive forces, limits

---

[*] Joseph Stiglitz speaking on the financial crisis and its causes at a public forum on March 6, 2009, in New York City, available at http://www.youtube.com/watch?v=OIxMQ3V0uc4.

on speculation (through excessive debt), and a variety of governmental policies (including regulations and taxes) typically prevent the accumulation of massive wealth by a few individuals. However, once a process of great wealth accumulation begins that takes advantage of some new mechanism for diverting wealth to a limited number of individuals, it becomes self-reinforcing: The people—and associated businesses—who are already benefiting from this wealth accumulation expand their activities and, if necessary, use their wealth to influence the political process and remove barriers to additional wealth creation. At the same time, a class of aspiring magnates sees the opportunities created by this first group and expands the use of whatever loopholes, corporate holding companies (as in the era of the 1920s), or financial engineering to further this process of wealth accumulation. Finally, the use of excess debt, speculation, and margin (the 1920s version of what we now call leverage) almost always plays a central role in this process. During periods where asset prices are rising, high debt levels allow aspiring magnates to multiply their earnings into the stratosphere. However, at some point the level of debt involved becomes unsustainable, asset values are overbid, and the system crashes.

In short, in certain cases, extreme inequality may be more than just one precursor to crisis. It may directly lead to the economic shock that is the final, key precursor. We don't need a terrorist attack: We are at critical mass already.

ADDED SIGNS OF DANGER

Economic inequality has also harmed the fundamental way members of our society relate to each other. Earlier, I discussed research that concluded that levels of trust were closely related to levels of economic equality. There is now strong evidence that trust in our society is rapidly breaking down. Scholars have identified several different types of trust, and levels for all appear to be approaching 30-year lows. The first of these is generalized trust within our society, which has been decreasing throughout the period that economic inequality has been increasing. The General Social Survey, a biannual assessment of American values, is widely regarded as the best source of information on societal trends. Between 1972 and 1980, the percentage of people who agreed that "most people can be trusted" (as opposed to "you can't be too careful in dealing with people") remained essentially constant. However, from 1980 to 2006, the percentage of people who generally trust others declined from 44 percent to 32 percent, the lowest level ever recorded by the survey.*

While more recent data is not available, it's almost a certainty that the economic crisis has exacerbated Americans' lack of generalized trust. In *The Moral Foundations*

---

* General Social Survey 1980–2006, available at http://www.norc.org/ GSS+Website/Browse+GSS+Variables/Subject+Index/.

of Trust, Eric Uslaner studied a wide variety of surveys conducted over the past several decades to determine why people trust each other. He concluded "If you believe that things are going to get better—and that you have the capacity to control your life—trusting others isn't so risky."[*] As the economic crisis emerged, so too did a widespread lack of optimism, spurred by a general feeling that many of society's institutions and leaders have betrayed the population (either for their own gains or because they were inept). All this has almost certainly pushed Americans' basic lack of trust in others to even deeper record lows. We now live in a society permeated by distrust.

Second, trust in the institutions that comprise our economy is critical to the maintenance of our financial system. In 1972, the Nobel laureate Kenneth Arrow wrote that "Virtually every commercial transaction has within itself an element of trust."[†] When we deposit money in a bank, we trust that it is safe. When a company makes an order, it trusts that it will be fulfilled. In describing the importance of trust, other scholars note that "it is an essential lubricant that greases the wheels of the economic system."[‡] Robert Reich, the former secretary of labor, writes that "When the history of the Mini Depression of

[*]   Eric M. Uslaner, *The Moral Foundations of Trust*, 33.

[†]   Quoted in *Measuring Trust, Introducing the Financial Trust Index*, *Kellogg Insight Focus on Research*, Kellogg School of Management, February 2009.

[‡]   Paolo Sapienza and Luigi Zingales, "Anti-Trust America: A Trust Deficit Is Driving Our Economy Down," *City Journal* (online), February 27, 2009.

2008–2010 is written by future historians, the word 'distrust' will appear again and again."[*] As the economic crisis has evolved, trust in financial institutions, U.S. companies, and government regulators has dropped precipitously.

Finally, in September 2008, Gallup's annual Governance poll found that trust in government institutions had tied its historic nadir of 1973, at the height of the Watergate crisis: Just 26 percent of Americans were satisfied with the way the country was being governed. Just 18 percent of Americans approved of the job Congress was doing. There are, of course, various measures of hopeful public opinion regarding the Obama administration, starting with the president's early, strong approval ratings. But the underlying, long-term trend has been toward lower and lower approval ratings for Congress and Washington as a whole.[†]

Anger in America is rapidly rising as well. There is a growing sense that middle- and lower-class Americans are suffering as a result of corporate incompetence, while incompetent businessmen have walked away with multimillion-dollar paychecks. Americans nearing retirement are angry as the home equity and

---

[*] Robert Reich, "Hope and Trust and the Mini Depression," Robert Reich's blog, February 20, 2009, http://robertreich.blogspot.com/2009/02/hope-and-trust-and-mini-depression.html.

[†] Gallup, "Trust in Government Remains Low," September 28, 2008, http://www.gallup.com/poll/110458/Trust-Government-Remains-Low.aspx.

stock savings they expected to fund their retirements are disappearing. Millions of responsible people, who face foreclosure because of lost jobs, high medical bills with no insurance, or other calamities, see the top echelons of corporate America continuing to receive enormous pay packages despite huge losses and the layoffs of thousands of employees. This anger is magnified by a growing sense that the wealthiest members of our society, those who have caused this suffering, don't appreciate the misery they have wrought—and will continue to enjoy a life of splendor. Robert Reich, the former secretary of labor, said it well when he wrote:

> Typical Americans are hurting very badly right now. They resent people who appear to be living high off a system dominated by insiders with the right connections . . . In short, many Americans who have worked hard, saved as much as they can, bought a home, obeyed the law, and paid every cent of taxes that were due are beginning to feel like chumps. Their jobs are disappearing, their savings are disappearing, their homes are worth far less than they thought they were, their tax bills are as high as ever if not higher.
>
> Meanwhile, people at the top seem to be living far different lives in a different universe. They're the executives and traders on Wall Street who have lived like kings for years off a bubble of their

own making while ripping off small investors, the financial louts who are now taking hundreds of billions of taxpayer bailout money while awarding themselves huge bonuses and throwing lavish parties, the corporate CEOs who are earning seven figures while laying off thousands of workers.[*]

Similarly, Frank Rich of the *New York Times* described "the populist rage coursing through America" and the "mounting public anger" at a "greedy bipartisan culture of entitlement and crony capitalism that both helped create our economic meltdown [on Wall Street] and failed to police it [in Washington]." Rich also described the simmering frustration in the public's mood, noting "Most 'ordinary Americans' still don't understand why banks got billions while nothing was done [and still isn't being done] to bail out those who lost their homes, jobs and retirement savings."[†]

Surveys of the American public released in March 2009 support the observations of Reich and Rich. The Pew Research Center found that almost half (48 percent) of Americans say they are "angry" about the government "bailing out banks and financial institutions that made poor financial decisions."[‡] During this same month, a furor erupted

---

[*]   Robert Reich, "Hope and Trust and the Mini Depression," February 20, 2009.
[†]   Frank Rich, "Slumdogs Unite!" *New York Times*, February 7, 2009.
[‡]   "Obama's Approval Rating Slips Amid Division Over Economic Proposals,"

over the payment of $165 million in bonuses to executives at AIG, a company that has been kept on life-support thanks to massive infusions of federal money. While the finance community seemed to regard bonus payments in excess of $1 million to 73 people[*] as business as usual, Gallup found that 59 percent of the American people feel personally "outraged" by the bonuses.[†] I believe the overwhelming public reaction to the AIG bonuses was, in reality, symptomatic of a larger issue: Americans were latching on to this incident as a way to express their growing anger and frustration with a system that rewarded, and continues to reward, the few who destroyed our financial system at the expense of everyone else.

The danger is that these emotions will turn increasingly ugly. If millions of people—who believe their anger is justified—lose their homes, jobs, retirements, and dreams, can we realistically expect continued loyalty to our system? In particular, how will angry people react if they feel their lives have been unfairly ruined for the benefit of a small number at the top?

Pew Research Center, March 16, 2009, http://people-press.org/report/498/obama-approval-slips.

[*] "AIG Bonuses 'Staggering' in Size, Seven Execs Received Over $4 Million Each," ABC News online, March 17, 2009, http://abcnews.go.com/Blotter/WallStreet/story?id=7102959.

[†] Gallup, "Outraged Americans Want AIG Bonus Money Recovered," March 17, 2009, http://www.gallup.com/poll/116941/Outraged-Americans-AIG-Bonus-Money-Recovered.aspx.

TERRORISM, TRIGGER POINTS, AND ECONOMIC INEQUALITY

This book opened with a fictional scenario involving terrorism and economic inequality. This leads to some natural questions: Does economic inequality make a society more vulnerable to terrorism, and does economic inequality even foster terrorism? In addition, the terrorists serve as the trigger point for political instability in the scenario. Does this have any special meaning?

Since the attacks on the World Trade Center, we have become conditioned to think about terrorists almost exclusively as individuals or groups pursuing an anti-American, Islamist agenda. Earlier in our history, America experienced repeated periods of violence in which the perpetrators had very different agendas, but this history has largely been forgotten. The renowned historian Richard Hofstadter wrote about this phenomenon, "the subject has been repressed in the national consciousness . . . Americans who came of age after the 1930s found it easy to forget how violent a people their forebears had been." Indeed, the first American terrorists were the Sons of Liberty who, led by Samuel Adams, carried out the Boston Tea Party in 1773.* Terrorists can be inspired by religious or political convictions. When political transformation is

---

* Hofstadter quoted in David C. Rappaport, "Before the Bombs There Were the Mobs: American Experience with Terror," *Terrorism and Political Violence* 20 (2008): 167–168.

the motivating factor, the goal of a terrorist group is to fundamentally alter a political system through violence where the specific act has psychological repercussions beyond the immediate target. Historically, the main goal of such terrorists was not to kill but to attract media attention to their cause in the hope of initiating reforms. This is the type of terrorism portrayed in the opening of the book.

The terrorist act is carefully crafted to create a message. It is designed to show the aims of the terrorists and to appeal to a "target audience." Left-wing terrorists have traditionally been inspired by, and attempted to draw attention to, the perceived inequalities of their state. While the damage they inflict is real, the main goal of such terrorists is a call to action for their political cause. In the fictional scenario at the start of this book, the terrorists actively worked to avoid injuring people, as opposed to property, for this reason. They were working to grab media attention for their cause while attempting to avoid public condemnation as murderers. As one expert has written, "For the terrorist, success in having this impact is often measured in terms of the amount of publicity and attention received. Newsprint and air-time are thus the coin of the realm in the terrorists' mind-set."*

Modern terrorism was made possible by the invention of dynamite by Alfred Nobel in 1866. "The new tool en-

---

* Bruce Hoffman, *Inside Terrorism* (Columbia University, 2006), 229, 247.

abled small groups, and even individuals, under the cover of surprise to frighten and influence masses, which is why the first modern terrorists virtually worshipped dynamite," notes one scholar.[*] From the so-called "Dynamite Club" of bomb-throwing anarchists in late nineteenth-century Paris, to the dynamite-wielding nihilists who tried to assassinate Tsar Alexander II several times before ultimately succeeding, all the way to the Red Brigades in Italy in the sixties and seventies, and the Weather Underground in the United States, dynamite has been a tool of choice. The horrible technological leap from dynamite to a dirty bomb is obvious. With a few dirty bombs, a small group can potentially create panic and chaos throughout a nation. Inevitably, this accomplishes one of the objectives of terrorists: They receive extraordinary amounts of media coverage. To the extent that the terrorist message resonates with a large segment of the populace, particularly in a sharply divided nation, their efforts will also focus the media on their political cause. To be sure, the success of non-state terror, no matter what era or form, is rare. One study of the efforts of Samuel Adams's Sons of Liberty concludes that this success stemmed from three factors: First, the cause was popular with the general populace. Second, the government was ambivalent about its own policies. Third, the rebels restrained themselves in terms of the violence they committed.[†]

---

[*]   Rappaport, "Before the Bombs There Were the Mobs," 167.
[†]   Ibid., 186–187.

It would be an understatement to say that we live in an era that is markedly different from the time of the founding American Revolution. Nonetheless, a key aspect of the success of the initial terrorist activity is the support of the populace. To the extent that extreme inequality and the financial crisis lead to increasing anger, suffering, and misery, our society will become both more divided and far more sympathetic and supportive of the aims of terrorists who oppose the privileges of a few while many are suffering. Moreover, our government will be caught defending a system that is obviously in need of serious repair. This framework succinctly answers our first question: In these circumstances, we will unquestionably be more vulnerable to terrorism.

A related question is whether extreme economic inequality makes a society more likely to foster terrorism. This is a difficult question, in part because only a limited amount is known about what causes an individual to become a politically motivated terrorist. I would contend that anything that fosters widespread anger, envy, and perceived subjugation increases the potential that some small group will use extreme and abhorrent methods to voice its rage. With growing inequality, far more people are likely to believe that the American Dream has failed them and become increasingly alienated from our society. An alienated group could, for example, develop a particular anger associated with a perceived hypocrisy between the vision of the American Dream (in which they were raised) and their perception of a divided society that offers limited mobility. If extreme inequality is combined with the collapse of high expectations, the potential for a group to lash out at perceived injustice becomes even higher. Finally, terrorists choose their actions based on their perceptions of potential success and popular support, and both of these are likely to grow stronger as suffering attributed to economic inequality increases. So, unfortunately, I conclude that extreme economic inequality does create a greater potential for terrorism from within the nation.

Understanding Trigger Points

The final question addressed here is whether there is any special meaning to using terrorists in the opening scenario as a way of triggering the revolution. In the fictional opening, the terrorists serve as the trigger point that hastens the collapse of the American government. The chapter on the theory of revolution consciously does not address trigger points. From one perspective, the actual trigger point or event that sets a revolution in motion is rarely consequential in itself. In this scenario, the use of the terrorists as the trigger point is entirely a fictional device. The reason trigger points are effectively irrelevant is that political instability reflects a broad confluence of social forces that develop over years or decades. Revolutions may seem like they come out of nowhere or officially start at a specific moment, but in fact they have, in almost all cases, been simmering and boiling below the surface for a very long time. It could be riots by foreclosure victims. It could be extreme political tensions between federal and state governments. It could be a new and different kind of terrorism altogether. Ultimately, the trigger is less important than the cascade it launches.

However, there is also a second perspective. As technology has advanced through human history it has become increasingly possible for fringe terrorist groups to exploit the divisions within a society. With knives or swords, a small group could only injure a limited number of people before it was eventually subdued. With the invention of dynamite, these same individuals could hurt more people. Dynamite also added a fearsome new element to potential terrorist strategies: bombs could be detonated remotely. As a result, terrorists no longer needed to be on-site at the time of an attack. Now, the potential to create dirty bombs (and perhaps biohazards) has added yet another element to the terrorists' arsenal: the ability to incite fear and panic on a scale that was simply not possible before these weapons existed.

If the central goal of a terrorist group is to attract media attention and force a society to take notice of the group's demands, then dirty bombs bring this capability to an entirely new level. As the scenario at the start of the book demonstrates, dirty bombs give terrorists the ability to command the attention of a nation. The most important function of a government is to keep the people safe. The difficulty in defending a nation against dirty bombs allows terrorists to potentially create an impression of government incompetence.

The precise trigger of a cascade of events leading to revolution is, ultimately, irrelevant. Triggers activate forces that have been building in the society for a long period of time, and are likely to burst one way or another. With dirty bombs, however, terrorists may be able to *accelerate* the impact of these long-term forces by bringing an unprecedented level of media attention, and consequently spreading mass fear. These in turn help reinforce the perception that the state is incompetent.

CHAPTER SEVEN

AMERICA IN A TIME OF VULNERABILITY

THE DANGER OF RISING EXPECTATIONS

Throughout recorded history, a central cause of the collapse of governance systems has been issues associated with the problem of rising expectations. As problems are recognized, a nation's leaders develop plans for reform and communicate these plans to an eager (and often long-suffering) public. Then, something happens that causes these reforms to fail. It is irrelevant whether the reforms were badly conceived at the outset or unanticipated events such as crop failures (as in the French Revolution) or the collapse of oil prices (as in the Soviet experience) led to new stresses on the society. When it becomes clear that a bedraggled nation has placed rising hopes for change in a failed effort, the resulting anger, increased stress throughout the society, lack of trust, and expectation of continued economic misery lead the government to fall. In the face of dashed expectations, the populace turns to some other means for revitalizing the society.

As this book goes to press, the first of what may be several emergency economic stimulus efforts during the Obama presidency has been in place for several months. The scale of this urgently needed effort is vast by traditional standards. Yet, many prominent economists believe this effort to restart the economy will fail because we are not spending enough. Public officials and academics now anticipate that unemployment will exceed 10 percent of the work force while those who are underemployed or too discouraged to seek work could encompass an additional 15 percent of the work force. The truth is that we are in uncharted waters and the possibility that our public policies will fail, *over the short or long term*, is very real. As former secretary of labor Robert Reich says, "We have never been here before." Reich, who testified on the early 2009 economic stimulus bill before Congressional lawmakers, put it bluntly, "If anybody tells you they know exactly what to do, don't believe them."*

The expectations for the Obama presidency are unreasonably high. Obama accedes to the presidency at a time of national crisis that has only been equaled by the

---

* "A Crisis Trumps Constraints," *New York Times,* January 7, 2009.

Civil War and the Great Depression. As a consequence, it's natural for the media to compare him to two of our greatest presidents, Lincoln and Roosevelt. This comparison is strengthened by his historic election as the first African American president, and the widely held perception that the "cycles of history" have turned with his accession to power. In combination with a Democratic majority in both houses of Congress, the election of President Obama is a strong repudiation of the politics of the past decades and has been seen as a revitalizing force in the nation.

This response is human nature. People need hope. They need something to grasp that says everything will turn out all right: President Obama's efforts are the recipient of all of these emotions.

However, this historic opportunity brings impossible expectations. We face a crisis with roots stretching back three decades. It is unrealistic to expect that the nation can return to business as usual in a short period of time.

Obama himself seems to recognize the impossibility of the expectations his election creates. During the campaign, he said that he wanted to be judged on his first 1,000 days in office, not his first 100.[*] Nonetheless, he faces a difficult balancing act. In order to gain approval for his massive efforts, he must show confidence that they will succeed. He is caught between the inevitable need to sell his plan and its benefits, and the danger that he will over-

---

[*] "First 100 Days as Crucial as New Deal, Says FDR Author," *Guardian* (U.K.), November 15, 2008.

sell the speed or certainty of success. What will be the public mood in 2010 if unemployment remains high or worsens? In *The Unthinkable: Who Survives When Disaster Strikes—and Why,* Amanda Ripley of *Time* magazine examines how people characteristically respond to disasters. While her study focuses on physical disasters, her discussion of the stages of reasoning associated with incomprehensible physical events seems equally applicable to all sorts of sudden, once-in-a-lifetime threats. Ripley argues that disaster victims start with "denial," which involves both *delaying* a response to the crisis and then *underestimating the risks* involved.[*]

Here's one demonstration of the public's high capacity for self-denial in this crisis: Despite all of the noise about declining housing prices, one study found that in the third quarter of 2008, half (49 percent) of all homeowners believed their home's value had increased or stayed the same during the past year. In fact, nearly three-quarters (74 percent) of all homes had actually *lost* value in the preceding 12 months.[†]

Americans can, by and large, be divided into three groups: (1) those who have lost their jobs, face foreclosure, or are otherwise suffering at this moment from the

---

[*] Amanda Ripley, *The Unthinkable: Who Survives When Disaster Strikes—And Why* (Crown, 2008), 1–14.

[†] Luke Mullins, "Many Homeowners Still in Denial about Prices," *U.S. News & World Report*: Money & Business Blog, October 31, 2008, http://www.usnews. com/blogs/the-home-front/2008/10/31/many-homeowners-still-in-denial-about-prices.html.

economic crisis in an immediate and tangible way; (2) those who are worried that they may lose their home or job in the coming months; and (3) those that are securely employed and housed, but have lost large chunks of their savings. Those who have lost their jobs or fear the loss of their jobs may also have suffered large losses in the equity markets. At the time of the stock market crash in October 2008, I received a large number of calls from friends and colleagues who said, "I now know I am never going to be able to retire." These callers were still in a state of shock and denial. They were talking, but did not seem to be making an effort to really come to grips with what had happened. Finally, one caller gave me a clearer sense of this attitude. He said, "It seems to me the new administration has to do something. They can't just let all these people who played by the rules lose their life savings. What about all those people in finance who are still sitting on tens of millions of dollars? I am going to try very hard not to feel anything until I see what Obama does."

So, here's my concern: I believe millions of people—primarily in the middle class—are facing a new reality: Their diminished lifestyle is leading them to real questions about their ability to live the American Dream. However, this segment of our society has collectively made a decision to hold its breath and look for magic from Washington. Rather than begin to accept what has happened, and is happening, they have remained in what Ripley describes as the "delusion" phase. There is no immediate physical threat to push them out of this delusion.

Their incomes remain (at least for the moment) in place.

For this reason, people have placed even greater expectations on what Obama can achieve. Rather than internalize the damage to their lives, a large chunk of our society has transferred its emotions to unrealistic hope that Obama can quickly change the course of our economy and the state of the markets. We may fervently hope that Obama is the next FDR or Lincoln, but if we are already holding him to that standard, the rising expectations meter is furiously blinking red.

We live in an age of instant gratification. Today's high debt levels are a testament to that fact. How often has it been said in the past few months that we are a nation of consumers as opposed to savers. Our consumerist society cannot help but look for a short-term solution to the economic crisis. Unfortunately, this short-term mentality created the problem in the first place.

The problem of the suffering middle class has been building for at least two decades. Until recently, the middle class borrowed heavily to maintain its lifestyle. Now, the decreasing pay scales—and availability—of middle-class jobs that are both white-collar and blue-collar can no longer be hidden through debt or rising home values. What was a struggling group has suddenly woken up to a sense of overwhelming hopelessness, combined with anger that this has been allowed to happen.

There is a very real danger that the Obama administration will, with the best of intentions, end up exacerbating the problem of middle-class anger. The administration has established a task force, led by Vice President Biden, to address middle-class issues. I fervently hope that this group is effective; however, the success rate of past government task forces designed to address broad or vaguely defined problems is not encouraging.

It is by no means clear that the Obama administration—or anyone else—has the answer to revitalizing the middle class. The plans discussed to date are designed to get the economy moving again, but are not going to reverse the trends discussed throughout this book. This will require a far more radical realignment of the way wealth is distributed within the society.

The problem is real. The solution is hard. The one thing we do know is that the government *must* create the belief that pain is being shared throughout the society: that the wealthy are—in a fair way—sharing in the suffering of the middle rungs of the national community.

Parallels to the Great Depression

There is a Depression-era equivalent to this problem, and it may well be where the Obama administration ends up. When FDR took office, the Depression was in full force, and there was a real fear of revolution emanating from the farmers as well as the working class. For example, in the winter of 1932–33, Edward O'Neal of the American Farm Bureau Federation warned Congress, "Unless something is done for the American farmer we will have revolution in the countryside in less than twelve months." Farmers' Union president John A. Simpson wrote to FDR, then president-elect, in January 1933, stating "that unless you call a special session of Congress . . . and start a revolution in government affairs there will be one started in the country. It is just a question of whether or not you get one started first."* This was also the only other era in which economic inequality rivaled the levels of today's society.

In many respects, the farmers were the equivalent of the middle class today. They had suffered prior to the Great Depression as a result of decreasing agriculture prices, while everyone else enjoyed an increasing prosperity. Farmers, like today's indebted middle class, had drawn heavily on their savings before 1929. They were frequently invoked as rhetorical cover for legislation, such as the Smoot-Hawley tariff, that ultimately hurt rather than helped them. As discussed earlier, numerous instances of armed violence broke out across the farm belt prior to FDR's inauguration.

Farm leaders warned that the farmer, who "is naturally a conservative individual," would revolt against a system that appeared increasingly unfair. In 1932, the president of the Wisconsin Farmers' Union testified before the Senate Agricultural Committee. He warned "The farmer is naturally a conservative individual, but

---

* McElvaine, *The Great Depression*, 92, 147.

you cannot find a conservative farmer today. I am as conservative as any man could be, *but any economic system* that has in its power to set me and my wife on the streets, at my age—what else could I see but red . . . They are just ready to do anything to get even with this situation . . . I honestly believe that if some of them could buy airplanes, they would come down here to blow you fellows all up."

Similarly, Edward McGrady, a representative of the conservative American Federation of Labor, testified before a Senate committee in the spring of 1932 that while the leaders of his organization had been "preaching patience," "I say to you gentlemen, advisedly that if something is not done . . . the doors of revolt in this country are going to be thrown open . . . It would not be a revolt against the Government but against the administration."* One of the ways FDR combated this risk was with increasing radicalism. He committed the government to attacking the Depression to such an extent that the downtrodden public identified with the White House and Washington. FDR's radicalism was evident in his acceptance speech for the Democratic presidential nomination in 1936:

> An old English judge once said: "Necessitous men
> are not free men." Liberty requires opportunity to
> make a living—a living decent according to the

---

* Arthur M. Schlesinger, Jr., *The Age of Roosevelt*, Volume I, *The Crisis of the Old Order: 1919–1933* (Houghton Mifflin, 1957), 174–176.

standard of the time, a living which gives man not only enough to live by, but something to live for.

For too many of us the political equality we once had won was meaningless in the face of economic inequality. A small group had concentrated in their own hands an almost complete control over other people's property, other people's money, other people's labor—other people's lives. For too many of us life was no longer free; liberty no longer real; men could no longer follow the pursuit of happiness.

In April 1936, *Time* magazine wrote of the "depth of this bitterness" the well-to-do felt for Roosevelt. The magazine wrote, "Regardless of party and regardless of region, today, with few exceptions, members of the so-called Upper Class frankly hate Franklin Roosevelt."[*] Roosevelt hence avoided political instability by paradoxically engaging in class warfare.

We are a different society today, and I am not advocating a return to the radical rhetoric employed by FDR. What I would suggest, however, is that the Obama administration needs not only to effect actual change, but also to *provide suffering people with the all-important perception that the president is unswervingly on their side.* Moreover, whatever rhetoric the Obama administration employs

---

[*] "Death of Howe," *Time*, April 27, 1936.

will only go so far. Suffering people will also expect that the president's executive and legislative activities live up to his rhetoric. At the end of the day, the president's programs must align with his words.

In the wake of the financial crisis, there are two pieces of information, discussed earlier, that prevent me from sleeping at night:

- The findings of a recent study that almost four out of five of all middle-class households (78 percent) lack the savings to survive for more than three months at three-quarters of their current spending levels. In essence, an estimated 78 percent of middle-class homes are living paycheck to paycheck.
- Experts project that eight to ten million families will face foreclosure in the next few years. These astounding numbers represent 15 to 19 percent of all mortgages in the United States.*

One shudders at the idea of millions upon millions of Americans who previously led middle-class lives losing their homes, their jobs, their remaining assets, and their sense that they share a stake in the outcome of our society. The difference between their expectations and this diminished reality is potentially dramatic and cata-

---

* Associated Press, "Housing plan aims to help 9M, but leaves out many," March 5, 2009 ("nearly 52 million US homeowners with a mortgage").

strophic. What we must recognize is that if the middle class is engulfed by the current economic tidal wave, the destruction of our democracy as we have always understood it will almost certainly follow.

No country in history has maintained a vital democracy without a vibrant middle class: Democracy and extreme income inequality are ultimately incompatible.

Democracies can fail because of paralysis. As decision makers become polarized, bold action can become impossible or necessary action is simply postponed for years or future generations. In *The Zero-Sum Society,* MIT economist Lester Thurow articulates why our democracy is exceptionally bad at making decisions that involve allocating resources between winners and losers.

Our inability to make difficult decisions is, in large part, one reason for many of our most pressing national problems, including our ballooning national deficit and our inadequate healthcare system. We repeatedly postpone hard choices.* Moreover, it can be argued that our nation adopted the policies that led to rising economic inequality because of the false belief that they would benefit everyone. Politicians and economists argued that the policy initiatives associated with the ideology of free-market exuberance, relying on the magic of minimally regulated markets and trickle-down economics, would increase the wealth of our entire society.

---

* Lester Thurow, *The Zero-Sum Society: Distribution and the Possibilities for Economic Change* (Basic, 1980), 12–16.

With a Democratic president supported by large democratic majorities in both houses of Congress, there is a natural tendency to assume that once again our democracy has self-corrected: Now Congress and the president will be able to get something done. However, both Jimmy Carter and Bill Clinton found that Democratic majorities did not necessarily provide for productive governance. Not all Democrats may agree to support particularly strong policy measures, and Washington remains a city with 14,000 active, registered lobbyists.*

There are many ways in which political polarization could ultimately lead to government incompetence in managing the economic crisis. Health insurance reform is one example of a problem for which the federal government has had many ideas but, to date, only failed solutions. And that's easier to solve than inequality. Indeed, as FDR contemplated his radical New Deal, it is worth noting how he addressed the prospective problem of polarization. We remember Roosevelt's first inauguration speech for his famous statement that we have "nothing to fear but fear itself." However, the portion of the speech that received the loudest applause was when FDR said that if necessary, he would seek all of the powers equivalent to a president in war to address the crisis. In effect, FDR was threatening the Congress: Follow my lead or I will do something more drastic.

---

*   "Former Lobbyists Join Obama," *National Journal*, January 24, 2009.

It is one thing to pass a tax cut or bail out a company. It is something else entirely to transfer wealth from the rich to the poor. No group has historically given up its privileges without a fight. As efforts to rebalance wealth within the society become critical, it would be natural for the wealthy to use their power and influence to attempt to maintain the status quo.

Indeed, Simon Johnson, a prominent MIT professor and former chief economist for the International Monetary Fund (IMF), argues that the bank rescue plan adopted by the Obama administration in the spring of 2009 was heavily influenced by oligarchs in the financial sector who were seeking to maintain their sources of wealth and power. In a blog post titled "High Noon: Geithner v. The American Oligarchs," Johnson asked the question:

> There comes a time in every economic crisis, or more specifically, in every struggle to recover from a crisis, when someone steps up to the podium to promise the policies that—they say—will deliver you back to growth. The person has political support, a strong track record, and every incentive to enter the history books. But one nagging question remains. Can this person, your new economic strategist, really break with the vested elites that got you into this much trouble?*

---

*   Simon Johnson, "High Noon: Geithner v. The American Oligarchs," Baseline Scenario (blog), February 8, 2009, http://baselinescenario.com/2009/02/08/

On a more theoretical level, Robert Dahl, the eminent Yale political scientist, warned in his 2006 book, *On Political Equality,* of an "ominous possibility" that once a particular group gained outsize political influence in the nation, "political inequalities may be ratcheted up, so to speak, to a level from which they cannot be ratcheted down."* In essence, Obama's overwhelming victory at the polls is no guarantee that his administration will have the clout, or the will, to successfully fight the entrenched interests that Teddy Roosevelt called "the malefactors of great wealth" who will inevitably oppose the strong policies necessary to reverse decades of rising economic inequality.

---

high-noon-geithner-v-the-american-oligarchs/; see also, Bill Moyers' Journal, February 13, 2009, transcript of Bill Moyers interview with Professor Simon Johnson, http://www.pbs.org/moyers/journal/02132009/transcript1.html; and Simon Johnson, "The Quiet Coup," *Atlantic,* May 2009.

* Robert A. Dahl, *On Political Equality* (Yale, 2006), 85.

BRINGING BALANCE TO OUR SOCIETY

I n the winter of 2009, riots swept across eastern Europe. The finance ministry of Latvia was attacked by a mob. Protests in Lithuania and Bulgaria turned violent. Greece had suffered widespread violence for months, sparked, in part, by low salaries and unemployment among the young. In western Europe, labor unrest was on the rise. Hundreds of thousands marched in France's major cities in January. Demonstrations occurred in Britain. Ireland teetered on the edge of bankruptcy, with hundreds of thousands taking to the streets. In Germany, autoworkers staged mass rallies.

In America, we read these headlines and we thanked God that it could never happen here. But from the Whiskey Rebellion in 1794 to the riots that spread from Watts to so many cities in the late 1960s and early 1970s, it *has* happened here. It's time to ask the question, What can we do to stave off potential revolution?

What follows is a general prescription of policies and

goals that will be necessary for us to undo the negative impact of the past 30 years. In essence, we must bring back what we have lost: a sense of trust in government and business institutions, an economy that fairly rewards productive citizens at all levels, a sense that benefits are equally shared, a vibrant middle class, and a revitalized American Dream.

To realize this goal, we must acknowledge two distinct principles. First, we need to recognize that our failed economics were based on an ethos that ultimately undermined the functioning of our society. Second, we must recognize that we cannot solve these problems through business as usual. When FDR proposed many of the cornerstones of today's economic system, programs ranging from FDIC insurance to social security, they were considered radical ideas that would undermine our capitalist society and individual responsibility. Today we see them as part of a safety net that helped save capitalism from itself. We must ask ourselves how we redefine basic institutions and rights to ensure that we emerge stronger as a nation.

The Failed Ethos of Free-Market Exuberance

After touring the United States in the 1830s, de Tocqueville presciently warned that while the essence of democracy as it existed in the United States was what we would call equality of opportunity, one of the inherent dangers in the system was that individuals would focus solely on their own well-being. In particular, he was concerned that the wealthy would focus solely on acquiring more wealth without regard to the well-being of anyone else or the society as a whole. He wrote, "There is, in fact, a perilous passage in the life of democratic peoples . . . Preoccupied with the sole care of making a fortune, they no longer perceive the tight bond that unites the particular fortune of each of them to the prosperity of all."* By and large, that is exactly what has happened in the late twentieth and early twenty-first centuries.

If we have learned one thing from the current economic storm, it is this: We are all connected. Whether I like it or not, my well-being depends on the well-being of my neighbor. If my neighbor's house goes into foreclosure, the value of my house decreases. If an abundance of people lack decent jobs, the economy goes into a tailspin, stock values decline, pension funds are diminished, and everyone suffers. We cannot build a lasting society that assumes greed is good and civic virtue is irrelevant. This is not a view derived from moral or ethical considerations. It is a view based on the empirical evidence of the past 30 years. It is also the analysis that motivated FDR's reforms. In his first inaugural address, Roosevelt also declared, "We now realize, as we have never realized before, our interdependence on each other."

We must restore both the perception and the reality

---

* De Tocqueville, *Democracy in America*, 515.

that as the nation prospers everyone prospers. This simple notion—that we are all in this together—is the underlying philosophy for the policy ideas detailed below.

These policies can be roughly divided into three categories: First, activities that are necessary to restore trust in the central institutions of government, finance, and business. Second, policies that provide a greater economic security for low- and middle-income households, what we might term a new safety net, or even basic rights, appropriate to our twenty-first-century economy. Third, a set of policies oriented toward reining in some of the excesses and abuses that evolved in the era of free-market exuberance. In essence, we can attack the problem by bolstering the lower and middle slices of the income pyramid and eliminating inappropriate largesse at the top.

Let's start with restoring trust in our central institutions. President Obama has entered office with the highest reservoir of goodwill of any new president in modern times. In contrast to the polarization that has ruled our politics over the past several decades, even some opponents are hoping for his success. Great crises can create a transformational moment in American politics where national priorities, the need for action, and pragmatism trump ideology and party bickering. Yet the expectations of the American people for what the Obama administration can accomplish seem impossibly high. The opportunity and dangers here are both high.

First and foremost, the Obama administration needs to be honest with the American people. During the Bush administration, it became commonplace to see denials of actions or events one week, and then, like clockwork, ultimate confirmation of those actions the administration had previously denied. As widely reported, Bush started to believe that he could, in fact, define his own reality. The American people demand better. With a fresh start, Obama has the opportunity to set realistic expectations by telling the American people what they can and cannot expect, and, most important, how quickly or slowly to expect it. It is far better for Obama to warn of a long difficult road ahead—while explaining the actions he is taking to ultimately succeed—than to promise quick success.

There is also the real danger that President Obama's strong rhetoric will not be matched by similarly strong action. Obama has acknowledged the deep problems in our society and promised strong action. As FDR demonstrated, words must be matched by deeds. A true source of catastrophe might be the mass conclusion by the middle class that despite President Obama's rhetoric, the world is continuing with business as usual, on the same path toward increasing inequality.

Second, a crucial part of restoring trust is action and communication. FDR had a well-known penchant for pragmatic action, to see what worked and what did not. We would like to believe that we can predict what will and will not pull us through this crisis, but as so many commentators have noted we are in uncharted waters, and anyone who tells you they know how this will come out is lying. The American people respond to action. And they will, I believe, accept the idea of experimentation, provided it is associated with three key elements: communication, transparency, and accountability.

Indeed, it can be argued that the Bush administration's late-term efforts to stabilize the financial system had all the danger that in past centuries ultimately led to revolution. The goals of the infamous Troubled Asset Relief Program (TARP) were unclear. How the money was actually spent has been subject to a scathing review by the TARP bipartisan oversight panel.* Most important, the general feeling of the American people was that the financial system was rapidly spinning out of control despite hundreds of billions poured into TARP. Little real effort was made to explain why plans were or were not succeeding as the process proceeded. In combination with a perception that the Bush efforts were ideologically biased in favor of wealthy people, TARP created a dangerous and potentially combustible brew.

As the new administration moves forward, *truthful education* and *communication* are critical components to rebuilding trust. The administration must take the time to explain what it is attempting to do, how it will help *all* Americans, and the means for evaluating progress along the way. Regular statements of progress, along a predictable time table, will help us through a difficult period. If presented correctly, people can accept slow

---

* "TARP Oversight Panel Urges Transparency, Accountability," *Wall Street Journal*, January 10, 2009.

progress. They can also accept an explanation that we tried some experiments, and not all of them worked— so here is what we are doing now and here is why we think it will work. The Obama administration will hit inevitable bumps on the road to building an economy that once again benefits all Americans, but the more people feel they are a part of the process, the less the chance of the calamities that can accompany failed expectations.

The ability to restore trust in business and the financial system is also essential for the long-term political stability of the nation. People become increasingly alienated from a system if they view it as unfair. They become far less committed to productive participation and far more likely to revolt in small and large ways. For example, many Americans who accepted credit card teaser rates did not know that they could ultimately be subject to annual rates exceeding 30 percent (plus flat late fees, making the effective interest rates even higher), which are now common. Some commentators have called this "Gotcha Capitalism."* It's legal—the terms were discussed in very fine print—but the consumer is tricked into a situation he or she would never have knowingly chosen. The consumer lending divisions of many of the banks we are now bailing out did everything they could to bury these potential fees in long, unreadable contracts. These same banks—who vigorously

---

* Bob Sullivan, *Gotcha Capitalism: How Hidden Fees Rip You Off Every Day—and What You Can Do About It* (Ballantine Books, 2007).

oppose modification of their mortgage loans—did everything they could to *lobby and manipulate the political process* in order to make credit card debt harder to discharge in bankruptcy. The resulting consumer preference for paying credit card debt over mortgage fees has been cited as one of the causes of the housing crisis.

(Speaking of which, do you know why most credit card bills originate in South Dakota or Delaware? Because unlike many other states they have no usury laws, which effectively means the United States as a whole operates without usury laws, rules that are fundamental to most religious and ethical systems.)*

If the financial crisis worsens I would not be surprised if consumers simply stop paying their credit card bills as a form of protest. Like the farmers in the Depression, these consumers would be acting on a belief that fundamental issues of fairness have been violated at their expense. On a mass scale—which is not impossible—this would cause untold damage to respect for institutions in our society. In a delicate system, this kind of protest could even serve as a trigger event for a larger protest against our basic economic structure.

Second, to restore trust in the business system, we need to maintain personal responsibility but we also need to eliminate—whether through regulations, laws, or government pressure on the banks—the most flagrant

---

* "Loophole Lets Rates Rise on Credit Cards," *Los Angeles Times,* February 18, 2009.

abuses of the system that are exacerbating the problems of the middle- and low-income classes, at the expense of the highest-paid sectors in society. Reforming credit card rates would be high on this list.

It's important to recognize that formal rules and regulations can only take us so far. We also need to establish a new ethos of what is, and is not, acceptable behavior. For example, in the 1950s a CEO who laid off workers would have been seen as a failure. Today, stock prices frequently rise when management announces employment cutbacks. Similarly, CEOs in the 1950s would have been embarrassed to receive salaries that are on average 270 times those of the lowest paid workers. In the era of free-market exuberance our ethos of responsibility to one another, which defined behavior, was subsumed by short-term profit motives, under the veil of a misinterpretation of Adam Smith's "invisible hand."

We must have a change in attitude: Simply because something is legal does not make it right or acceptable. Wall Street is full of colorful words and phrases that bankers use to indicate that they have "unloaded" a package of assets of questionable value. For example, a *New York Times* page one story describes a lawsuit involving a Wall Street practice of advising one "valued client" to purchase a complex security, while advising other clients to invest against this type of security—as it would surely

lose money.* Average individual investors and home buy-
ers are often unaware of the extent of conflicts of interest
associated with the people they are trusting for advice.
Moreover, there is no question that many of the problems
of the current crisis result from short-term actions that
the participants knew would be financially rewarding in
the near term but were bad for the long term.

The new ethos for business must be one of individual
responsibility and accountability. Our business leaders
must create an environment that says we do not celebrate
or condone activities that while legal are harmful to the
customer or the society. Many of the excessive salaries
that have led to income inequality have also resulted
from precisely this kind of activity.

Gresham's law, a widely quoted truism related to currency, holds that "bad money drives out good." In our era,
an appropriate law of money might be that "speculation
and excess move outside of regulation." If freedom is the
ability to do whatever you want *without hurting anyone
else,* then it is an appropriate role for government to assure that the financial industry is not putting any of us at
risk. In the financial arena, excess income inequality and
the economic crisis resulted from the same set of activities: unregulated financial activities that were effectively
vast speculative efforts, made easier by governmental bias
toward waiving, eliminating, or failing to enforce exist-

---

* "After Sure-Bet Investment Fails, a Bank Contends It Was Duped," *New York
Times,* January 19, 2009.

ing regulations—on the assumption that the free market would police itself. We now know the obvious: People will take enormous risks with other people's money in order to earn enormous fees. Ultimately, these activities led to short-term profits (accompanied by enormous salaries), and far larger longer-term losses and destruction of value.

The Nobel laureate George Akerlof and Yale economist Robert Shiller have used the phrase "animal spirits" to describe this type of predictable excess. They note that, "History—including recent history—shows that without regulation, animal spirits will drive economic activity to extremes."[*]

To restore trust in our financial sector, the American people need to know that they are protected from egregious speculation that puts their savings and prosperity at risk. This will require both new regulations and the vigorous enforcement of rules that are on the books but have been largely ignored. A related objective must be the development of compensation systems that fairly reward people for value they create over the long term. It has now been well documented that in many, many cases, top corporate executives can earn tens of millions of dollars even when their companies perform poorly. Corporate boards have failed in their responsibility to demand accountability and to oversee appropriate pay

---

[*] George A. Akerlof and Robert J. Shiller, "Good Government and Animal Spirits," *Wall Street Journal*, April 23, 2009.

systems.* A wide range of studies have demonstrated that this excess pay is not necessarily correlated with improved corporate performance. The American people support enormous rewards where fairly earned—principally in the entrepreneurial arena. However, the perception that pay for public company executives has simply gotten out of hand—even as these same people head companies that are shedding employees right and left— could actually serve as a further trigger to political instability. The pay of public company officials is publicly reported, and as the suffering of the nation increases so will a sense of outrage—or even worse.

I don't have the solution to fixing corporate governance. It is a complex subject. But we must recognize that the system is broken. A reformed system must accomplish the following: (1) ensure that executive pay is truly aligned with the long-term value created for the company—as opposed to short-term results, (2) impose far greater accountability on corporate leaders, (3) vocally adopt a new operating ethos, which recognizes that while some decisions may be legal that does not make them acceptable or desirable, and (4) reexamine the star system of executive pay that has led to astronomical salaries of questionable value.

The next piece of any plan to address economic inequality and ensure political stability must embrace poli-

---

* See, for example, Lucian Bebchuk and Jesse Fried, *Pay Without Performance: The Unfulfilled Promise of Executive Compensation* (Harvard, 2006).

cies oriented toward economic security, and ensure the survival of the middle class and the American Dream:

First and foremost, we must keep people in their homes. The loss of millions of more homes will increase anger, alienation, and despair throughout our society; potentially represent a death blow to the middle class; and substantially increase the risk of political instability. At the start of 2009, one of every nine homes with a mortgage was either behind on mortgage payments or in the foreclosure process, and one in every five homes with a mortgage was underwater (the mortgage was higher than the value of the home).* With few exceptions, every estimate of the depth of the calamity now confronting the U.S. economy has *understated the actual damage and risk.* Without dramatic government action the total number of foreclosures could be even higher than these seemingly consensus estimates.

Yes, the prudent buyer may resent that his imprudent neighbor next door is receiving government assistance. However, we are all connected. The problem should never have been allowed to arise in the first place. Now that it has, the prudent next-door neighbor will also be worse off if multiple homes on his or her block are foreclosed. Moreover, the loss of a home is often the first step in an ever-worsening downward spiral. Today's resentful

---

* "Report: 1 in 5 Mortgages Are Underwater," BusinessWeek.com, March 3, 2009, http://www.businessweek.com/bwdaily/dnflash/content/mar2009/db2009033_306801.htm.

neighbor may be unemployed tomorrow if massive foreclosures continue and even accelerate.

There are a wide variety of ways the government could move to ensure people keep their homes, and I will not attempt to lay out a specific policy proposal here. However, it is certainly worth noting that drastic action on this front was a central, although often less remarked-upon, aspect of the New Deal. In 1933, Congress created the Home Owners Loan Corporation (HOLC), which bought up mortgages and ultimately owned one in every five mortgages in America.* Most of us don't realize that this agency also helped to create the standard 30-year mortgage that served America well for so long. Prior to the Depression, mortgages typically ran as short as five years. HOLC bought mortgages and offered homeowners refinanced, fully amortized 15-year mortgages at lower interest rates. In part, the financial innovation associated with buying up five-year mortgages and re issuing them for longer 15-year terms saved home ownership for millions of Americans. The uniform appraisal methods adopted by HOLC along with the creation of the Federal Housing Authority (FHA) (established in 1934 to insure long-term mortgages in a manner similar to the FDIC bank deposit insurance) ultimately made private lenders comfortable in offering 30-year loans.† We must develop a similarly bold strategy in our own era.

---

* Alan Blinder, "From the New Deal a Way Out of a Mess," *New York Times*, February 24, 2008.
† Kennedy, *Freedom from Fear*, 368–370.

As he led the nation through a violent revolt, Lincoln similarly recognized the need for strong, bold actions that reformed the inadequacies of the old order. This extract from his second annual message to Congress in December 1862 is equally applicable to our present situation: "The dogmas of the quiet past are inadequate to the stormy present. The occasion is piled high with difficulty, and we must rise with the occasion. As our case is new, so we must think anew, and act anew. We must disenthrall ourselves, and then we shall save our country."

Second, for many workers, one of the most frightening aspects of job losses today is the associated loss of health insurance for themselves and their families. This problem is undoubtedly a symptom of the larger healthcare problem that confronts the nation: As a nation, we spend twice as much in GNP on healthcare as the average OECD country, but rank twenty-eighth in life expectancy according to the World Health Organization, on par with Portugal and just above the Czech Republic.[*] These out-of-control costs threaten the future of Medicare and undermine the economic security of all but the wealthiest Americans. In fact, our healthcare system is now so dysfunctional that even health insurance can be insufficient to protect a family's finances. One prominent study found that a medical crisis was a leading cause of bankruptcy, and three-quarters of the

---

[*] See "America's Health Rankings" (based on *World Health Statistics 2008*), http://www.americashealthrankings.org/2008/othernations.html.

medically bankrupt had health insurance at the onset of the crisis.*

Do you really believe that the greatest nation on earth can survive in its current form without providing decent healthcare to its citizens, when every comparable society does? The health insurance crisis is part of the larger healthcare crisis. We cannot provide a lasting health insurance solution without solving the underlying problem. Nonetheless, at this moment, we can ensure political stability by adopting one of many ideas for broadening the health insurance access available to Americans, with subsidies as necessary. Once this system is in place, the government will have an even greater incentive to attack the underlying problem of runaway healthcare costs.

Third, we need to recommit ourselves to ensuring the mobility that is fundamental to the American Dream. The promise of America is that everyone will have the equal opportunity to realize his or her potential. Today, America is less mobile than the majority of European nations, and Americans are increasingly feeling that we are a divided nation of haves and have nots, as opposed to a fluid society full of opportunity for all. There are undoubtedly multiple reasons that mobility has decreased, but unequal access to education is high on the list. College completion rates are markedly higher as students move up the economic spec-

---

* See Elizabeth Warren, "Sick and Broke," *Washington Post*, February 9, 2005.

trum. As a consequence, a recent article in *Harvard Maga-zine* concludes, "Compared to the mid-twentieth century, higher education is now increasingly exacerbating socio-economic inequality in the United States."[*] Moreover, one likely result of the financial crisis is that middle-class fami-lies (particularly those in the $40,000 to $60,000 range) will be increasingly unable to afford college.[†]

America's colleges are the envy of the world. Yet many of our elementary and secondary schools are shameful. We must also have public schools that work. This may seem as intractable a problem as solving healthcare. There is strong evidence that aspects of the housing bubble were caused by families that bid up, and overspent, on homes located in school districts of perceived higher quality. At this macro level, the housing bubble, the subsequent bust, and our current economic peril can, in part, be traced to the shortage of quality public schools. As daunting as it may seem, educational reform must be at the cornerstone of a serious effort to address economic inequality.

Finally, let's discuss tax policy. While we are at re-cord levels of economic inequality, we are also at record low levels—for the modern era—of tax rates. Contrary to modern mythology, the connection between higher tax rates and decreased work and productivity is tenuous at

---

[*] "Reopening the Doors to College: The Crisis in Access to Higher Education, and a Strategy for Moving Beyond Elite Handouts for the Lucky Few," *Harvard Magazine,* March–April 2009.

[†] See, for example, "Middle Class Families in the $40,000 to $60,000 Range May Not Be Able to Afford College," *Sun-Sentinel* (Florida), February 24, 2009.

best. Indeed, far higher tax rates prevailed in the 1950s through the 1970s, which witnessed the greatest boom in U.S. productivity and growth.

Tax policy also involves the larger question: At what point is it appropriate to ask the most fortunate citizens to pay a higher share of the costs of maintaining a prosperous society? At this point, our society is out of balance: Massive income inequality and massive economic dysfunctions have jointly placed us all in danger. In this context, it seems appropriate to ask for a greater contribution from the only slice of the income pyramid that has grown significantly over the past several years.

In recent years, low capital gains taxes have been one of the principal ways individuals have amassed extraordinary fortunes. Yes, there is merit in a low tax to spur investment in starting new businesses. But there is also a point where the lower tax ceases to serve as an incentive. Moreover, almost all of the beneficiaries of this tax are the nation's wealthiest citizens and many are investing in ways they would pursue regardless of this tax preference. As a consequence, I would suggest that a higher capital gains tax rate is appropriate. A higher rate would balance the valuable incentive provided by this tax preference, the need to raise government funds, and the disproportionate wealth this tax preference has allowed many individuals at the very top end of the income scale to amass.

Finally, there is undoubtedly room to create a more progressive tax system without discouraging work or the accumulation of income. However, I am going to leave that argument for another day. The appropriate tax rates need to reflect the overall needs of the society, which it is impossible for me to assess here. At the same time, I would suggest that we should do everything we can as a society to address the issue of income inequality before the tax system is employed for this purpose. If we start with the tax system, we are effectively saying that the goal is to redistribute money to a society where income inequality is inevitable. I reject the notion that we cannot do better in the way we arrange work and compensation in the society itself.

CONCLUSION

As I have been working on this book, and discussing it with friends and colleagues, I have often been asked some variation of this question: "You aren't really serious about the revolution, are you? Isn't it really just a gimmick to get people to pay attention to the issue of inequality?" I certainly hope the discussion throughout this book has made it clear that the answer is emphatic— this is no gimmick, I am very serious. But perhaps one last word is in order for any possible doubters who remain.

The Great Depression brought violence to America. There was a rise of ugly populism, stoked by people like Huey Long and Father Coughlin. There were violent labor strikes. There was a bonus march of World

War I veterans, who crossed the country to the District of Columbia demanding compensation for their wartime service, until they were forcibly cleared out (with several casualties) by General MacArthur and the army. Whether or not Marine Corps Major General Smedley Butler, who supported the Bonus Marchers and was one of the most popular military figures of his day, actually contemplated a coup to overthrow Franklin Roosevelt remains a persistent, if minor, debate among historians. In the end, there was no true revolutionary movement in 1930s America. The United States escaped the Depression thanks to violence, but it was the violence of World War II rather than a civil war.

What we face today is every bit as challenging as the Great Depression. Furthermore, the means to destabilize the country are greater than ever, thanks to the existence of terrible weapons that could be obtained by any number of radical fringe actors. I cannot sufficiently underscore that this book is intended as a wake-up call, a warning, by a writer who loves his country. It is precisely because I do think the threat is very real, and that we have reached a historically unprecedented position of social weakness, that I began this book with a worst-case scenario. We cannot rest easier even if, soon, the credit markets are functioning well, the housing market recovers, and unemployment eases. We have been placing untenable stress on the middle class for too long, through boom times and recessions, for economic recovery to be the only answer to our ills. We face a deep crisis, and we all need to see it, and react to it, and change our worldview if we are to emerge as strong as we have been in the past.

Certainly, we all share that goal. Will we change our thinking in order to achieve it?

INDEX